Psychotherapy without the Self

Psychotherapy *without* the Self

A Buddhist Perspective

MARK EPSTEIN, M.D.

Yale University Press   New Haven & London

Published with assistance from the foundation established in memory of
Philip Hamilton McMillan of the Class of 1894, Yale College.

Set in Minion type by Keystone Typesetting, Inc.
Printed in the United States of America.

Library of Congress Control Number: 2007923909
ISBN: 978-0-300-12341-8

A catalogue record for this book is available from the British Library.

The paper in this book meets the guidelines for permanence and durability
of the Committee on Production Guidelines for Book Longevity of the
Council on Library Resources.

10   9   8   7   6   5   4   3   2   1

To Arlene, Sonia, & Will

"The great Buddhist scholar D. T. Suzuki came to Columbia to teach [in 1951] and I went for two years to his classes. From Suzuki's teaching I began to understand that a sober and quiet mind is one in which the ego does not obstruct the fluency of things that come in through our senses and up through our dreams. Our business in living is to become fluent with the life we are living, and art can help this."

—*John Cage*

Contents

Acknowledgments

This book was greatly enhanced by the opportunities I have had to teach with Robert A. F. Thurman and Sharon Salzberg. Working with them has been a wonderful education in its own right. I am similarly grateful to Joseph Goldstein, Jack Kornfield, Stephen Batchelor, Daniel Goleman, Jeffrey Hopkins, Emmanuel Ghent, Michael Vincent Miller, and Michael Eigen for their unflagging support for my work. Keith Condon and John Donatich at Yale University Press, and Anne Edelstein, brought this book into its current form. I also thank my patients, who have shared their lives, thoughts, and feelings with me, enriching my life and my work tremendously. In the few instances where case studies appear, I have changed names and other identifying details or constructed composites in order to protect privacy.

Introduction
Toward a Buddhist Psychotherapy

I have long been interested in the issue of psychological change. Immersed in Buddhism before beginning my study of Western psychiatry and psychotherapy, I could not help but examine the Western therapeutic approaches that were taught to me in college and medical school through the lens of the East. How consistent were they with what the Buddha taught? I wondered. Could Western psychologies be compatible with a Buddhist psychology that questioned the very reality of the self?

As I learned more and more about the psychoanalytic traditions of the West, I came to appreciate that in their own way they too question the ultimate reality of the conventionally appearing self. I also began to reflect upon how these Western traditions could help me to understand the processes of mental development charted by the great Buddhist psychologists of the past several millennia and modeled for me by the Buddhist teachers I had come in contact with. As I learned more about Buddhism, I came to appreciate that its central tenet of *anatta*, or no-self, does not mean what I had initially assumed it to mean. The Buddha did not dispute the relative reality of the conventionally appearing self. But he did insist that we tend to give this relational self an absolute status that it does not possess. We think that it is more real than it is, and we expend an extraordinary amount of energy propping it up and protecting it, reinforcing the certainty of our own separateness. Both psychotherapy and Buddhist meditation have the potential to undo this tendency, relieving us of our defensive loads. In these chapters I insist that they can work together to sharpen our understanding.

Going back and forth between East and West has allowed me a great luxury. Simultaneously immersed in each, I have been tethered by neither. Instead, I have been able to question, as both traditions encourage, some of the basic assumptions that drive our understanding of the self. Can we transform ourselves? How does psychic change happen? Is therapy necessary? Does meditation alter personality or character? What does psychological healing really mean? The chapters in this collection chart the development of my own thinking as I have written a series of books about psychotherapy from a Buddhist perspective. They reflect the issues I have wrestled with as I have tried to puzzle out the relationship of meditation to psychotherapy, a relationship just at the dawn of its own evolution.

In the earliest series of chapters included here (grouped under the heading "Buddha"), originally articles written in the 1980s for the California-based *Journal of Transpersonal Psychology,* I looked at Buddhist psychology from a psychodynamic stance, thereby contributing to a translation process that Buddhism has had to go through every time it moves into a new culture. As Buddhism merged with the nature psychology of Taoism in China, for instance, it gave birth to the new form of Ch'an, or Zen, Buddhism. Similarly in the West, our understanding of the psyche is entrenched in the psychoanalytic tradition, whose basic assumptions and vocabulary about the self have permeated our society. In order for Buddhism to be understood by our culture, it must be reinterpreted in the psychological language of our time. These early articles contributed to that process, taking such basic Buddhist concepts as egolessness, emptiness, the spiritual path, and the Four Noble Truths and discussing and defining them in psychodynamic language, opening up the potential for cross-cultural exchange. They were my own attempt to clarify what I had learned from Buddhism. What I came to appreciate was that the very attempt to interpret my understanding also helped to sharpen and clarify it.

The next set of chapters (grouped under the heading "Freud") were my first attempts to reach out to broader audiences to show how a Buddhist understanding of mind could be integrated with prevailing systems of thought in the West. Originally articles, some were written for psychoanalytic audiences and were designed to introduce Buddhist psychology to those clinicians who were drawn to, but perhaps wary of, the spiritual psychology of the Buddha. Others were written for those already familiar with Buddhism but more wary of Western psychiatry and psychotherapy, people struggling with issues of whether medications like Prozac or emotions like desire and anger could have a place in a Buddhist path. These chapters show the many parallels between the analytic, psychiatric, and Buddhist traditions and use Buddhist psychology to support and reinforce emerging trends in analytic theory that question the existence of a unitary, enduring self. They lay the foundation for an eventual integration of Buddhist and Western psychologies: the possibility of a mindfulness-based psychodynamic psychotherapy, a psychotherapy that does not take recourse in an absolute, enduring self but that does not deny the sufferings of the self as it conventionally appears.

The third set of chapters (grouped under the heading "Winnicott")—one article written for an international conference on the place of religion and psychoanalysis in the twenty-first century; another, an outgrowth of my book *Open to Desire,* dedicated to the memory of my dear friend, the psychoanalyst and composer Emmanuel Ghent; and others for presentation to gatherings of artists and curators interested in the interface between Buddhism and contemporary art— describe the paradigm shifts that the intersection of Buddhism with Western culture has evoked. From the making of art to the practice of psychotherapy to the appreciation of intimate relations, the Buddhist influence creates the possibility for both new understandings and new misunderstandings. These chapters, as a group, are the most recent of my writings. They reflect the influence of the work of the British child analyst D. W. Winnicott, whose musings helped pave the way for an interest in Buddhism and an acceptance of alternative models of psychic health by contemporary psychotherapists and their patients.

In the West, or at least in what we think of as the psychologically minded West, one of the most prevalent models of psychological health is of the person who is willing to go deeply into his or her own problems. This model even influences the way many Westerners approach meditation, imagining, as they do, that they should explore the dark sides of their personalities—their fears, anxieties, depressions, and conflicts —while sitting on their meditation cushions. Hidden within this view of mental health is a kind of secret agenda—one that has to do with establishing a sense of certainty about the self, as if it could be known, or exposed, completely; as if we could dig down, as Freud wished, through the archaeological layers of the self to its roots in order to know it absolutely. Analysis, in this way of thinking, is something that can be directed by the conscious mind, aided in its quest by the analytic tools of free association, transference, and dream interpretation.

Yet in Buddhism—and even in some more recent psychoanalytic schools—there has emerged a different model, one that is less about digging and more about opening. At the root of this difference lies an alternative view of the unconscious. In the classical Freudian view, the unconscious is the repository of forbidden urges and instincts, the awareness of which extends and completes the self. In the Buddhist view, the unconscious represents the potential for enlightened consciousness, the latent knowledge that the self that we normally take to be so real has only relative, not absolute, reality. As Adam Phillips has written, in his analysis of the correspondence between Freud and his colleague and student Sandor Ferenczi, Ferenczi succinctly anticipated this other model. "The patient is not cured by free-associating," Phillips wrote about Ferenczi's view, "he is cured *when he can free-associate*." Ferenczi's perspective moved in a more Buddhist direction: he felt that healing depended more on a shift in consciousness than an uncovering or resolution of conflict. Free association, for Ferenczi, became an end as well as a means.

There is a famous Tibetan story about a woman named Manibhadra that makes much the same point (Shaw, 1994, p. 22). A householder who was nonetheless engaged in an advanced meditation practice known as tantra, Manibhadra attained enlightenment while carrying water from the village well back to her home. Dropping her pitcher one day and seeing the water gush out of the broken gourd, she was suddenly liberated. The broken pitcher served as a powerful model of what her meditation was trying to show her. Like the water breaking forth, her consciousness flowed out and merged with all of reality. This jarring loose, or breaking free—this going to pieces without falling apart—is what Buddhism acknowledges as one of the self's secret needs—to be released from a belief in its own absolute reality.

These two models of change—the one of digging and the other of breaking open—are currently in competition in our culture. The desire for self-certainty rubs up against the need to let go. These chapters make the case for a Buddhist corrective to our Western drive for self-certainty and chart a course of integration where psychotherapy can still be imagined, even without the constraint of an intrinsically abiding self. The Buddha anticipated this discussion in one of his most famous teachings in which he dramatically refused to talk about most of what he knew. His teachings, he insisted, were just a "handful of leaves," tiny in comparison to all the leaves of the forest, to all that he had seen and understood. But they were all that were necessary for liberation, and therefore all that he would talk about. Like a good psychotherapist, the Buddha knew when to keep quiet.

To extrapolate upon the Buddha's insight, Buddhism teaches that it is not how much you know about yourself, it's *how* you relate to what you *do* know that makes a difference. This is a point that one of my American Buddhist teachers, Joseph Goldstein, has made to me over and over again when leading retreats that I have been to. "It's not *what's* happening to you or in you," he would insist, "it's *how* you relate to it that matters." The common tendency, Buddhism teaches, is to use whatever is happening to reinforce a distinct feeling of self: to take everything very personally. The alternative, as discerned by the Buddha, is to hold that very feeling of self up for critical examination whenever it arises. How real is this feeling that drives us, which we ordinarily take so much for granted?

Of the few leaves that the Buddha did display, the ones he talked about most often came to be known as the Four Noble Truths. When I was first learning about Buddhism, I traveled to Thailand with several of my friends and teachers and went to the forest monastery of a renowned meditation master named Achaan Chah. Gathering around him after our arrival, we asked him to explain the Buddha's teachings. He motioned to a glass sitting to one side of him. "Do you see this glass?" he asked us. "I love this glass. It holds the water admirably. When the sun shines on it, it reflects the light beautifully. When I tap it, it has a lovely ring. Yet for me, this glass is already broken. When the wind knocks it over or my elbow knocks it off the shelf and it falls to the ground and shatters, I say, 'Of course.' But when I understand that this glass is already broken, every minute with it is precious."

There is a lot in this story about Buddhism and what it has to offer to Western psychotherapy. The First Noble Truth comes through loudly and clearly: ordinary life, even pleasant and rewarding ordinary life, is tinged with a sense of pervasive unsatisfactoriness because of how fragile and transient everything is; the glass is already broken. The Second Noble Truth is also evident, that clinging to an idea of perfection or permanence or of an absolute, unchanging reality is the cause of suffering. The Third Noble Truth, that there is a kind of happiness not dependent on controlling the outcome of things, came through in the peace of mind that Achaan Chah was modeling for us. And the Fourth Noble Truth, known as the Eightfold, or Middle, Path, was also implicit in his response. Changing the way we relate to what happens to us and in us makes a different relationship possible with transience and fragility. This change in perspective can be practiced and learned; it allows us not to retreat into nihilism or indulge mindlessly in materialism, but permits us to enjoy the preciousness of the glass while we have it. It is this positive stance that is essential to Buddhism and, I believe, is the source of much of its appeal to the West.

But there is another interpretation of Achaan Chah's parable, one that relates to the way we experience the self, which is also of potential interest to the psychotherapist. Ordinarily, we assume that our feelings of having a self mean that the self is utterly real: unbreakable, enduring, permanent, and absolute. "Really real," as Professor Robert Thurman likes to say. But the Buddhist understanding is that, although the self appears to be real, it is only the appearance that *is* real. The self is not a lasting entity in its own right. It is not separate and distinct from the circumstances that give rise to its appearance. Understanding this crucial distinction enables one to enjoy the self's manifestations without trying to make them more than they really are. The glass can be valued, even treated as precious, while knowing that it is already broken.

While Freud had only glancing contact with the Buddha's psychology, he would have been sympathetic to the succinctness and coherence of his thought. He certainly understood, as the Buddha did, the mind's potential to both obscure and enlighten. His own aspirations were less global than the Buddha's, or Achaan Chah's, but they were marked by a similar economy. He famously remarked, for instance, that the best he could do with psychoanalysis was to bring someone from a state of neurotic misery to one of common unhappiness. He developed a number of strategies designed to elude the ever vigilant, and fearful, ego, including hypnosis, free association, dream analysis, and the analysis of transference, all of which he hoped to use to dig down into the archaic underpinnings of the self. In his reliance on techniques that could circumvent the rational mind, it was as if he were always searching for something like meditation. By the end of his life, though, Freud became frustrated with the limitations of psychoanalysis and began to talk of it as interminable. Perhaps to free himself from this dilemma, Freud turned his attention to a "death drive" that he named for the Buddhist nirvana. Balancing his earlier focus on eros, he saw in his death drive an urge to destruction or disintegration that seemed to parallel his understanding of the Buddha's definition of nirvana. The Buddha's ideas cast a spell on Freud, but he did not have a true understanding of the word he appropriated.

Nirvana was the Buddha's way of describing the freedom he found when he saw through the mirage of the self, the freedom that Achaan Chah was also trying to communicate in his parable about the glass, recognizing its preciousness while knowing that it was already broken. The Buddha's nirvana is not a drive toward death or disintegration, as Freud naively assumed; it is an ability to accept death and disintegration without falling apart; without twisting, distorting, or tormenting the mind in response. While nirvana once connoted "freedom from rebirth" in South Indian cultures where the endless rounds of death and reincarnation could seem even more interminable than a lengthy psychoanalysis, the freedom that the Buddha taught might more accurately be described as the ability to maintain one's composure in the face of an impermanent, always changing, and apparently imperfect, world (Epstein, 2001, pp. 121–126). While it was most certainly a psychological achievement, nirvana also suggested an underlying reality, one that could be uncovered, or opened to, by those willing to take seriously the Buddha's handful of leaves.

In this way of understanding, nirvana came to represent the freedom that is possible when the self is no longer clung to as an absolute entity. The freedom of nirvana is the freedom that emerges when self-centeredness is no longer organizing reality.

Freud, it seems, was in search of what the Buddha taught. Dreams, jokes, hypnosis, free association, and transference all undermine the sense of a separate, distinct, and unitary self. They take us from our habitual states of consciousness and move us to somewhere less structured, less sure, and less fixed. Yet Freud did not quite grasp the Buddhist unconscious. He mistook nirvana for disintegration and death. It was left to a later generation of psychoanalysts to come a little closer to the Buddha's stance.

In particular, the British analyst D. W. Winnicott moved therapy from a focus on unacceptable instincts and urges to a focus on the unintelligible aspects of emotional experience. "We are poor indeed if we are only sane," he remarked once in a famous footnote. Winnicott had the idea that the opposite of integration (the state of an apparently cohesive self) is not disintegration but something he termed *unintegration*. Here he was moving away from Freud and toward the Buddha. He compared unintegration to what it is like for a child to surrender himself in play, knowing that his mother is in the next room providing what he called "good-enough ego coverage." He also compared it to a lover's consciousness "after intercourse," when the urges are relaxed and the mind and heart are open, and to an artist's mind when unburdened in the studio. He saw the state of unintegration as the foundation of creativity and wrote volumes about the consequences of failing to tap into it. When a child has to manage an intrusive or ignoring parental environment, Winnicott suggested, he or she is forced to develop a "false" or "caretaker" self, centered in the thinking mind, in order to survive. This false self (which can paradoxically seem "really real") is created at the expense of unintegration, and the capacities for spontaneity, subjectivity, and authenticity are all compromised as a result. Winnicott, in his own way, seemed to be describing something akin to how the Buddhist unconscious could be covered over by early experience.

In bringing, in this book, a psychodynamic light to bear on Buddhism and a Buddhist light to bear on psychoanalysis, I hope to further the dialogue between the two. While Freud and Winnicott were two of the pioneering psychoanalysts of the past hundred years, the Buddha may have been the greatest psychoanalyst of them all. It is a happy accident that his teachings survive in the present day, ready and able to engage with the psychodynamic traditions of the West. Through the quirks of my own personal history, I was in a position to appreciate the words of the Buddha before beginning my official training as a psychotherapist. This work charts the course of my own progress in understanding how the two worlds fit together. It may be read with an eye toward how the confluence of the two traditions helped one therapist envision the exhilarating possibility of surrendering the false self.

References

Mark Epstein (2001). *Going on Being.* Boston: Wisdom.

Adam Phillips (1996). *Terrors and Experts.* Cambridge: Harvard University Press, p. 102.

Miranda Shaw (1994). *Passionate Enlightenment.* Princeton: Princeton University Press.

PART ONE

Buddha

The following four chapters, written as articles in the aftermath of my psychiatric residency, were inspired by my previous immersion in Buddhist thought and practice. The theoretical basis for them, on the Buddhist side, was the study of the traditional Buddhist psychology called *Abhidhamma*, which I undertook for my undergraduate thesis in psychology at Harvard. The experiential basis was a series of silent two-week *vipassana* retreats under the auspices of American Buddhist teachers Jack Kornfield and Joseph Goldstein that I took between 1974 and 1982. These chapters represent my first attempts to combine a psychodynamic way of thinking with one steeped in Buddhist psychology, and they grew out of my efforts to explain to myself, in psychological language, what I had learned from my study of Buddhism. At the time, in the mid-1980s, a consensus was emerging in the California-based transpersonal psychology movement that spiritual development was something that best took place on a platform of psychological development; that psychotherapy, if it was necessary at all, could most effectively be seen as a prelude to spiritual work. This point of view was most cogently summarized by the psychologist Jack Engler. "You have to be somebody before you can be nobody," he wrote at the time (Engler, 2003, p. 35).

Engler was responding to a disturbing trend noted by him and others: Western students of Eastern spiritual traditions who jumped into intensive meditation with little preparation sometimes experienced emotional distress. Many sincere practitioners, disillusioned with therapy or with the idea of therapy, turned to meditation in the hope of healing psychological issues and found that emotional material was uncovered that neither they nor their meditation teachers were prepared to deal with. Engler correctly noted the prevalence of borderline and narcissistic pathology in many of those drawn to meditation and proposed that psychotherapy was a better course of treatment for those having trouble maintaining a cohesive sense of self. Not only were analytically trained therapists better versed in the kinds of pathology such people suffered from, they were also trained in therapeutic techniques, knew how to handle transference issues, and were committed to the long-term one-on-one explorations helpful for such conditions. Buddhist teachers, on the other hand, whether of Eastern or Western backgrounds, were most often untrained in therapy, unprepared for the kinds of extreme distress that could emerge in Western practitioners, and uninterested in maintaining long-term personal relationships with students who might attend a workshop or retreat. Engler sought to remedy this very real problem by proposing that meditation was a kind of meta-therapy, appropriate for those who had already worked through the developmental tasks of selfhood, but inappropriate for those who had not yet done their psychological homework.

While this formulation was extremely helpful in exposing a very real problem, it never seemed completely right to me. Engler, in a later paper, has come to question it himself (Engler, 2003). In my own experience, meditation helped me come to grips with various narcissistic issues *before* I had any real therapy, helping me to become *somebody*. And therapy, far from promoting a strong and stable sense of self as envisioned by many schools of ego psychology, taught me how to let go, allowing me to be *nobody*. Many of my friends and acquaintances in the Buddhist world, some with a deep understanding of selflessness, still showed lots of evidence in their personality structures of borderline, neurotic, and narcissistic pathology, just as my psychiatric colleagues, many of them excellent therapists, did in their own personal lives. Spiritual communities were hotbeds of transference pathology, and many spiritual teachers, albeit highly realized, seemed just as vulnerable to acting out with their students as some therapists who could not help sleeping with their patients. It seemed incorrect to infer that those who were capable of Buddhist realizations of voidness or selflessness must be, by definition, psychologically intact or developmentally realized.

In a recent chapter, Engler (2006) has continued to rethink his original formulation, beginning his piece with an exchange between Phillip Kapleau, a respected American Zen master, and a student:

QUESTIONER: But doesn't enlightenment clear away imperfections and personality flaws?

ROSHI: No, it shows them up! Before awakening, one can easily ignore or rationalize his shortcomings, but after enlightenment this is no longer possible. One's failings are painfully evident. Yet at the time a strong determination develops to rid oneself of them. Even opening the Mind's eye fully does not at one fell swoop purify the emotions. Continuous training after enlightenment is required to purify the emotions so that our behavior accords with our understanding. This vital point must be understood. (pp. 29–30)

As Engler makes clear, this vital point is not what most people want to believe.

The result is a kind of guilt in many Western practitioners over the persistence, and continuing subjective importance, of their emotional lives. As Engler puts it, "The Buddhist teaching that I neither have nor am an enduring self should not be taken to mean that I do not need to struggle to find out who I am, what my desires and aspirations are, what my needs are, what my capabilities and responsibilities are, how I am relating to others, and what I could or should do with my life. Ontological emptiness does not mean psychological emptiness" (2003, pp. 34–35).

In my experience, therapy and meditation, psychological development and spiritual realization, seem to be intertwined. One can facilitate the other, or retard the other, or subtly infuse or contaminate the other. Realized beings can still be competitive, or narcissistic, or vulnerable to transference projections. Troubled, neurotic individuals can still be capable of profound insight. I wrote these articles to tease out a more nuanced view of the interplay of psychological, emotional and spiritual life. My ultimate position was that both "somebody" and "nobody" are falsely reified positions that do not do justice to what it means to be a person or to grapple with self. The Buddhist path of meditation, it seems to me, creates the conditions for subtler and subtler confrontations with narcissistic issues rooted, developmentally, in pre-verbal, infantile experience. And therapy, when practiced from a Buddhist perspective, seems just as capable of yielding liberating insight into the nature of self as meditation can be. But both methods must confront the truth of what Margaret Mahler once wrote, that the narcissistic residue "reverberates throughout the life cycle," (1972, p. 333). Or, in the virtually immortal words of Samuel Beckett, "The old ego dies hard, such as it was, a minister of dullness, it was also an agent of security" (quoted in Foster, 1989, p. 93).

References

Jack Engler (2003). "Being somebody and being nobody: A reexamination of the understanding of self in psychoanalysis and Buddhism," in Jeremy Safran (editor), *Psychoanalysis and Buddhism: An Unfolding Dialogue,* Boston: Wisdom, pp. 35–100.

Jack Engler (2006). "Promises and perils of the spiritual path," in Mark Unno (editor), *Buddhism and Psychotherapy Across Cultures,* Boston: Wisdom, pp. 27–40.

Paul Foster (1989). *Beckett and Zen,* London: Wisdom.

Margaret Mahler (1972). On the first three subphases of the separation-individuation process. *Int. J. Psycho-Anal.,* 53, 333–38.

I

Meditative Transformations
of Narcissism
(1986)

Attempts by theorists of transpersonal psychology to explain the place of meditation within an overall framework encompassing Western notions of the development of the self often see meditation as a "therapeutic" intervention most appropriate for those possessing a "fully developed" sense of self. This approach has been useful in distinguishing transpersonal levels of development from early, pre-oedipal levels, but appears to have sidestepped the issue of how Buddhist meditation practice, for example, could be seen as therapeutic for psychological issues that have their origin in the infantile experience of the meditator. The emergence of object relations theory and the psychodynamics of narcissism have provided a vocabulary more relevant for the discussion of such influences than was Freud's original drive theory that stressed the evolution and persistence of unconscious (Russell, 1986) aspects of libido and aggression. It has been noted that some of those attracted to meditation have demonstrable narcissistic pathology (Epstein & Lieff, 1981; Engler, 1983; 1984), but the role of meditation in *transforming* narcissistic pathology has not yet been explored. By focusing on two particular dynamic structures relevant to narcissism, the ego ideal and the ideal ego, and charting how these psychic structures are affected by the meditative path, it is possible to begin to unravel the complex relationship between meditation and narcissism.

Somebody/Nobody

Transpersonal theorists, in general, have preferred to portray the meditative path as beginning with an already developed sense of self, as progressing onward from where conventional Western personality theory leaves off. This approach asserts that Eastern psychologies pay relatively little explicit attention to the infantile components of the personality and that the transformation that they promise consists primarily of proceeding beyond the limitations of an already cohesive self. First delineated by Wilber (1980) in his descriptions of the "pre/trans fallacy," made explicit by Engler (1983; 1984) in his comparison of psychoanalysis and Buddhism, and finally codified by Wilber (1984a; 1984b) in his recent papers, this view is expressed most succinctly by Engler in his statement, ". . . you have to be somebody before you can be nobody" (Engler, 1983, p. 36). Such an orientation has proven to be an effective balance to the heretofore prevailing psychoanalytically influenced view that mystical states in general fostered a regression to pre-oedipal levels of fulfillment, yet it has, I believe, obscured inquiry into the question of whether Buddhist meditation practices could, in any way, aid in the resolution of infantile, narcissistic conflicts. When conceived as an either/ or perspective, the pre/trans rationale does not easily allow for the examination of the infantile matrix or developmental roots of the spiritual experience, nor does it readily demonstrate how inherent narcissism is engaged and continually addressed throughout the meditative path. In classifying Buddhist meditation practice as an "ethnopsychiatric discipline" (Engler, 1983), one must be open to the possibility that such practices may be confronting primitive psychological conflicts with an eye toward resolving them, not through "analysis," but through experiences in meditation that ultimately allow such conflicts to be transmuted.

Engler indicates there is a sizable proportion of individuals with demonstrable narcissistic pathology who seem to be drawn to meditation. He also describes their tendencies to form transferences to their teachers, often paralleling those described by Kohut (1971) in the treatment of narcissistic personalities. Yet he seems to feel that it is an anomaly of Western culture that individuals with narcissistic vulnerabilities tend to gravitate to the spiritual disciplines. I suspect, however, that this tendency is not unique to this culture and that its existence suggests an underlying thrust of the spiritual disciplines toward the resolution of narcissistically tinged issues (Masson, 1980).

This is not to assert that those individuals functioning at a clinically defined borderline level of personality organization (Kernberg, 1975) could withstand the rigors of intensive meditation practice. Indeed, the available evidence suggests that they cannot (Epstein & Lieff, 1981). In this respect I agree with Engler's conclusions regarding a "prerequisite level of personality organization." Yet his conclusions could also imply that the meditative experience, in a developed form, does not address infantile issues, that the ego must be "well integrated" and "intact" and its development "normal" for the meditative experience to unfold. Such a view might foreclose the use of the therapeutic potential of the meditative experience, or ignore the infantile origins of the attraction to spirituality, and neglect the narcissistic residue that may persist throughout the meditative path.

To assert that infantile issues can persist in their influence in the meditator's psyche even after he or she has successfully traversed the early developmental spectrum is not to contradict the major theorists of personality development, all of whom assert that the infantile residue "reverberates throughout the life cycle" (Mahler, 1972, p. 333). Those who have addressed narcissistic issues tend to agree on the essential point that the memory of the infant's blissful symbiotic union with the mother creates an ideal in the individual's psyche which inevitably becomes compared with his or her actual experience (Mahler, 1972, p. 338; Jacobsen, 1964, p. 39; Kohut, 1966, p. 246; A. Reich, 1960, p. 311; Guntrip, 1969, p. 291; Chasseguet-Smirgel, 1975, p. 6). This ideal is narcissistic at its core because it is rooted in a time when all of the infant's needs were immediately satisfied and when its self was not differentiated from that of its caretaker. Just as this narcissistic residue reverberates throughout the life cycle, affecting goals, aspirations and intimate interpersonal relationships, so it can be seen to reverberate throughout the meditative path, where psychic structures derived from this infantile experience must be, at various times, gratified, confronted or abandoned.

The concept of the ideal is not limited to the psychology of narcissism, however. One of the distinctive characteristics of Buddhist psychology (particularly in the Theravadan tradition) is that it clearly postulates an ideal personality, the *arahat,* that represents the fruition of meditation practice (Johansson, 1970; Goleman & Epstein, 1983), as well as an ideal state, that of *nirvana,* where reality is perceived without distortion. The ideal personality is conceived of as one in whom even the potential for the arising of unwholesome mental factors, such as greed, hatred, conceit, envy or doubt, does not exist. It represents a personality cleansed of the kinds of mental states accepted as inevitable by Western psychology—cleansed by virtue of the repeated experience of the enlightened state. In order to actually reach this goal, the meditative path, as well outlined in traditional Buddhist texts, must be traversed. From the perspective of the psychodynamics of narcissism, in order for this ideal to be reached, there must occur a transformation of those psychic structures that embody the individual's internalization of the ideal. In other words, meditation must inevitably affect those aspects of the self that derive from the infantile experience of the ideal so that the Buddhist ideal may be realized. It is not just that the promise of *nirvana* speaks to a primitive yearning and motivates some people to undertake meditation, but that the actual practice provides a means whereby those narcissistic remnants that inevitably persist are seized and redirected. The manner in which this occurs can be explained, once the psychic structures involved are described more fully.

Ego Ideal/Ideal Ego

The two representations of the ideal that inherit the energy of the infant's primitive narcissism (Grunberger, 1971) have been termed the ego ideal and the ideal ego (Hanly, 1984). They both derive from the infant's experience of undifferentiated, symbiotic fusion with the mother that predates cognitive structures mature enough for conceptual thought, but, once established, each assumes separate and distinctive functions within the developing individual's psychic economy. The *ideal ego* is "an idea which the ego has of itself" (Hanly, 1984, p. 254), an idealized image of what the ego actually is, a secret, tenaciously guarded, deeply held belief in the ego's solidity, permanence and perfection. The *ego ideal* is that towards which the ego strives, that which it yearns to become, that into which it desires to merge, fuse or unite. It is as if the original fusion with "mother and the sensori-physical surround" (Wilber, 1984a, p. 89) splits into two archaic, disjointed remnants, one embodying the ego's memory of its own perfection and the other embodying the memory of the perfection in which it was once contained. These two remnants diverge, at times contradict each other, and assume separate functions thereafter. They essentially constitute what has been termed the "dual orientation of narcissism" (Andreas-Salome, 1962).

> The fundamental difference between the two terms "ideal ego" and "ego ideal" is that the former connotes a state of being whereas the latter connotes a state of becoming. . . . The ideal ego is the ego insofar as it believes itself to have been vouchsafed a state of perfection—it refers to a positive state even if this state, in reality, is an illusion. In fact, the ideal ego is a self-image that is distorted by idealization but it may be experienced as more real than the ego itself. The ego ideal refers to a perfection to be achieved, it refers to an unrealized potential; it is the idea of a perfection towards which the ego ought to strive. (Hanly, 1984, p. 253)

The ideal ego, according to Hanly (1984), is the source of abstract ideas that the ego has about itself as perfect, complete, immortal and permanent. It is the wellspring of vanity and self-righteousness, the "source of an illusory ontology of the self" (p. 255) and the equivalent of a "wishful concept of the self" (Sandler et al., 1963, p. 156). It is given form when the ego gains the capacity to observe itself, when it senses its own presence (Federn, 1952, p. 60), yet its formation is "built up out of denials" (Hanly, 1984, p. 266) of many of the ego's attributes. Sustained by the on-going denial of what Federn (1952) has termed a "sense of unreality" or "estrangement" (p. 61) that arises when the "preceding state of perfect wholeness" (p. 269) is forever lost, the ideal ego does not permit inquiry into potentially contradictory aspects of the ego's true nature (Hanly, 1984, p. 260). The self, as experienced by the ideal ego, is not the constantly changing series of "fused and confused" self and object images that Jacobsen (1964, p. 20) described in her pioneering study of object relations theory, but is, instead, "an identification of the self with a part of the self which then becomes the 'true self' idealized by narcissistic investment" (Hanly, 1984, p. 255).

The ego ideal, on the other hand, embodies an individual's aspirations. It is derived from the boundless experience of infantile narcissistic omnipotence, in which there is no distinction between self and other and the entire universe is experienced as a part of oneself. First brought into existence by the "violent end to which the primary state of fusion" (Chasseguet-Smirgel, 1975, p. 6) is brought, the ego ideal is characteristically projected outward either onto significant others into which an individual tries to merge or into moral attributes which the individual tries to live up to. Yet, as Freud

(1914, p. 116) first stated, "That which he projects ahead of him as his ideal is merely his substitute for the lost narcissism of his childhood—the time when he was his own ideal." Unlike the ideal ego, whose function it is to assure the self of its own inherent perfection, the ego ideal is associated with a yearning to become something that at its root is an internalized image of a lost state of perfection. The ego ideal, says Chasseguet-Smirgel, a French psychoanalyst responsible for much of the repopularization of the concept, represents "a narcissistic omnipotence from which (the individual) is henceforth divided by a gulf that he will spend the rest of his life trying to bridge" (1975, p. 7).

Hanly (1984, p. 256) described the usefulness of these concepts in elucidating personality structure by comparing the relative strengths of ego ideal and ideal ego in various types of personality organization. His essential thesis is that relative strength of ideal ego and weakness of ego ideal predominate in borderline, narcissistic and neurotic disorders and that only as the personality matures does ego ideal begin to eclipse ideal ego in the psychic economy. This schemata assumes special importance as the fate of ego ideal and ideal ego in the meditative path is examined.

Attempts by psychoanalytic theorists to analyze mystical phenomena have traditionally resulted in interpretations that view meditation as a narcissistic attempt to regain an ideal infantile state. From early investigations of mystical ecstasies (Jones, 1913, 1923; Schroeder, 1922; Alexander, 1931; Federn, 1952) to Freud's well-known evocation of the "oceanic feeling" as a "restoration of limitless narcissism" (1930) to more contemporary attempts at describing mystical union (Rose, 1972; Ross, 1975; Lewin, 1950; Bonaparte, 1950; Masson, 1974, 1980), the essential point has always been a variation on the idea that mysticism in general and meditation in particular represents an attempt to merge ego and ego ideal, an idea first proposed by Jones (1923) and fully amplified upon by Grunberger (1971) and Chasseguet-Smirgel (1975). "Mysticism . . . corresponds . . . to the need for the uniting of ego and ideal via the shortest possible route. It represents fusion with the primary object, and even when the latter is represented consciously by God, it is nonetheless, at depth, an equivalent of the mother-prior-to-the-loss-of-fusion" (Chasseguet-Smirgel, 1975, p. 217).

With regard to the Buddhist path, this interpretation is but a half-truth, and, as such, it is revealing, incomplete and misleading. Such a formulation, while asserting that meditation strengthens the ego ideal, neglects both the fate of the ideal ego and the practices that affect the ideal ego. As psychoanalyst Joseph L. Thompson, writing under the pseudonym Joe Tom Sun in 1924 and the first analyst to appreciate this dimension of Buddhism, pointed out, "Buddha taught that the ego was not a reality, that it was non-existent, that it was an illusion" (Sun, 1924, p. 43), that the ideal ego, as a potent force in the psyche, must be surrendered.

The analytic view, traditionally, has been that meditation constitutes a regression to an infantile narcissistic state, a shortcut in the ongoing attempt to gratify the ego ideal. It is correct in pointing out that the potential for such gratification does exist through meditation, but, by failing to recognize the confrontation with the ideal ego that is also required, it has not recognized that restructuring of both ego ideal *and* ideal ego is demanded by the meditative path. On the other hand, transpersonal psychologists may not have recognized sufficiently the persistence of narcissistic structures in those undertaking meditation, and so may have overlooked the fate of those structures from an analytic point of view.

Concentration/Insight

As has been well described elsewhere (Nyanamoli, 1976; Goleman, 1977; Goleman & Epstein, 1983; Nyanaponika, 1962;
Brown, 1986), Buddhist literature contains a series of highly
systematized texts of psychological thought that detail not only
the varieties of day-to-day mental states but also how the con-
figurations of those mental states can be re-patterned through
the application of meditative techniques. Called Abhidhamma
in the Theravada school, these texts provide a detailed cartography, in phenomenological terms, of the psychological effects
of sustained meditation practice; they outline the substance
of the meditative path. Goleman (1977) has clearly described
the traditional Buddhist division of meditation techniques
into "concentration" and "insight" practices. Concentration
practices stress the development of one-pointed attention to
a single object, inevitably producing concomitant feelings
of tranquillity, contentment and bliss that can culminate in
absorption, or trance, states. Insight practices depend on
an attentional strategy called "mindfulness" that stresses the
moment-to-moment awareness of changing objects of perception. In this practice, attention is developed such that thoughts,
feelings, images, sensations and even consciousness, itself, can
be observed as an endless fluctuation characterizing the human mind and body process. A series of insights into the
temporary, unstable and impersonal nature of the personality
are said to occur as the path of insight is traversed, culminating
in the experience of enlightenment.

What is not so often emphasized, once this distinction is
accepted, is that the Buddhist meditative path demands a deli-
cate interplay of the two techniques and consists of a series of
alternating plateaus that reflect the affective concomitants of

first one strategy and then the other. While the development of the concentration practices to their limit is seen variously as a diversion or as a stepping-stone to more advanced insight practices, the development of concentration, and the feelings associated with it, also constitute an essential part of the technique of mindfulness and the path of insight.

Concentration allows the mind to remain fixed, without wavering, on a single object such as a sound, sensation, image or thought. Mindfulness allows attention to a rapidly changing series of objects but, as such, demands a sufficient degree of concentration to facilitate that process. Mindfulness combines the relaxed tranquillity of the concentration practices with an active, alert scrutiny of the field of consciousness that gradually matures into insight. Indeed, when the path of insight is analyzed carefully, stages with predominantly two contrasting affective tones can be discriminated, what the *Visuddhimagga,* the classic textbook of Buddhist psychology, calls experiences of "terror and delight" (Nyanamoli, 1976, p. 765).

The experiences of delight are essentially derived from the concentration practices or from the stabilizing elements of the mindfulness practice. They are characterized by feelings of contentment, harmony, tranquillity, bliss, rapture, expansiveness, wholeness and delight. They promote stability, equanimity and equilibrium and are essentially anxiolytic in that they directly counteract mental states of anxiety, worry and restlessness and evoke a state of well-being. These states may be associated with sensations of bright light, feelings of unlimited love or compassion, or bodily feelings of rapture or bliss. The precise configuration of these mental states depends upon where in the meditative path the individual happens to be, on which factors are most developed or most refined; but the thread that binds all of these states is clearly the delight elicited by the development of concentration. Within the traditionally outlined meditative path (Nyanamoli, 1976; Brown, 1986), the stages of delight are most pronounced at the levels leading up to and including what is termed access concentration, in the series of eight *jhanas*, at the level of pseudo-nirvana, and at the stages surrounding knowledge of contemplation of dispassion (see Figure 1).

The experiences of terror, on the other hand, derive from the investigating aspects of the mindfulness practice and from the insights that precipitate out of such practice. They are characterized by clear perception of the impermanent, insubstantial and unsatisfying nature of the self and the field of experience. These experiences are profoundly disturbing; they evoke discomfort, fear and anxiety, require the meditator to relinquish fundamental beliefs and identifications, and tend to be fragmenting and anxiogenic. They can only be withstood and tolerated if the counterbalancing forces of concentration are sufficiently strong. These are the experiences that Western psychologists fear will unbalance those with inadequate personality structures; yet from the Buddhist perspective equilibrium is maintained by the stabilizing effects of concentration. That such concentration might also solidify ego development could be explained by the identification of concentration with gratification of the ego ideal.

While the stages of delight must be worked through— they can prove so satisfying that it becomes difficult to move beyond them—the stages of terror must be continuously integrated. The meditator often receives the first inkling of terror at the very beginning of meditation, when confronted with the tumultuous nature of his own mind. As the concentration practices gradually calm the mind, this sentiment usually fades, only to resurface as mindfulness begins its investigation of the process of mind. As mindfulness develops the ability to discriminate successive moments of awareness, the emphasis is usually first on noting the successive arising of new mind moments. These perceptions begin to shake the foundations of what is termed "false view," that is, the identification of the individual with the products of his own psyche. As insight develops, the emphasis becomes increasingly shifted to awareness of the dissolution of each mind moment, and the stages of terror become more pronounced. The meditator experiences "all formations" continually "breaking up, like fragile pottery being smashed, like fine dust being dispersed, like sesamum seeds being roasted, and he sees only their break-up" (Nyanamoli, 1976, p. 752).

Following this stage, known as the Contemplation of Dissolution, comes a more intense realization, known as the Knowledge of Appearance of Terror, in which the threat to the ego is most vivid.

> As he repeats, develops and cultivates in this way the contemplation of dissolution, the object of which is cessation consisting in the destruction, fall and break-up of all formations, then formations classed according to all kinds of becoming, generation, destiny, station, or abode of beings, appear to him in the form of a great terror, as lions, tigers, leopards, bears, hyenas, spirits, ogres, fierce bulls, savage dogs, rut-maddened wild elephants, hideous venemous serpents, thunderbolts, charnel grounds, battle fields, flaming coal pits, etc., appear to a timid man who wants to live in peace. (Nyanamoli, 1976, p. 753)

It is here that the experience of terror is most raw and visible.

The division of the meditative path into experiences of terror and delight is instructive when considering the fate of the narcissistic psychic structures of ego ideal and ideal ego. The concentration practices clearly promote unity of ego and ego ideal by encouraging fixity of mind in a single object. Such fixity allows the ego to dissolve into the object, to merge with it in a suffusion of bliss and contentment extremely evocative of the infantile narcissistic state. Hindu practices, most of which are of the concentration variety (Goleman, 1977), are, in their own literature (Masson, 1980), said to bring about states most comparable to mother-child union. These are the practices conventionally referred to by analytic investigators of mysticism and described by Freud in his vision of the oceanic feeling. Alexander (1931) remarked on the similarities of a newly translated Buddhist description of the second *jhana,* or state of absorption, to the then evolving theory of narcissism and implied how such practices could gratify the demands of the ego ideal.

> This phase of positive attitude towards the ego is described in the Buddha text in the following words: "In this condition the monk is like a pool, fed from a source within himself, which has no outlet . . . and which also is not replenished by rain from time to time. This pool is fed from the cool stream of water within itself, with cool water streamed through, filled and flooded entirely, so that no single corner of the pool remains unsaturated: just so does the Bhikku drink from his physical body, fills and saturates himself completely from all sides with the joy and pleasureable feelings born out of the depths of absorption, so that not

the smallest particle remains unsaturated." This is the second jhana step. I think no analyst can more fittingly describe the condition of narcissism than is done in this text, if we substitute the word "libido" for "stream of water." For this reason this description seems to me especially interesting and important, because it is the description of a condition which we have only theoretically reconstructed and named "narcissism." (Alexander, 1931, p. 134)

The experience of terror, however, and the fruits of the insight practices, have little to do with the ego ideal. There is no satisfaction of a yearning for perfection in these experiences, no evocation of grandeur, elation or omnipotence. Rather, these experiences directly challenge the grasp of the deeply buried and highly treasured ideal ego. They confront the "illusory ontology of the self" (Hanly, 1984, p. 255), expose the ego as groundless, impermanent and empty, and overcome the denials that empower the wishful image of the self. When faced with these experiences, the meditator has nothing to fall back on; he must surrender his most closely guarded identifications, relinquishing them as "not me" and "not mine." As described in the *Visuddhimagga,*

> He sees the non-existence of a self of his own . . . he sees of his own self too that it is not the property of another's self. . . . He sees the non-existence of another's self, thus 'There is no other's self anywhere.' He sees of another that that other is not the property of his own self thus 'My owning of that

> other's self does not exist.' So this mere conglom-
> eration of formations is seen . . . as voidness of self
> or property of a self. . . . (Nyanamoli, 1976, p. 763)

Thus, the idealized image that the ego has inevitably held of itself since its infantile origins must now be extinguished, an event that is without parallel in Western dynamic theory.

The meditative path profoundly affects both residues of infantile narcissism. The ego ideal is strengthened while the ideal ego is diminished. These effects directly counter the prevailing intensities of the two that are thought to character-ize the pre-meditation, immature personality organizations, where ideal ego outweighs ego ideal (Hanly, 1984).

In the meditative tradition, the emphasis is continually on balancing the forces of concentration and insight, as if the stabilization and gratification of the former allows one to withstand the destabilization of the latter. Even at the thresh-old of enlightenment, what is said to be required is the simul-taneous arising of "concentrated absorption and appreciative analytical understanding" (Guenther, 1974, p. 139), the two processes that have been cultivated up until that point. It is as if the ego ideal must be sufficiently assuaged in order for the hold of ideal ego to be lessened. At the point where absorption and insight precisely balance each other, allowing the full dis-cernment of the voidness of self, the meditator is able to move beyond all residues of the ideal, beyond the last vestiges of narcissism, and into the experience of enlightenment. "Seeing nothing to be taken as 'I' or 'mine' . . . (the meditator) aban-dons both terror and delight" (Nyanamoli, 1976, p. 765), fi-nally leaving behind the remnants of ego ideal and ideal ego. It is not until this point that the psychic structures of narcissism lose their potential force.

INSIGHT

CONCENTRATION: Normal Waking Consciousness — 1st Signs of Concentration — Access Concentration — 8 Jhanas (Trance States or Absorptions)

Beginner's Sign
Learning Sign
Counterpart Sign

Four Form Jhanas
Four Formless Jhanas

Purification of View
(Insight into moment-to-moment processes)
|
Overcoming of doubt
(Succession of arising of objects noted)
|
Pseudo-Nibbana
Ten Imperfections of Insight
(Illumination, knowledge, rapturous
happiness, tranquillity, bliss, resolution,
exertion, assurance, equanimity, attachment)
|
Knowledge of Contemplation of Dissolution
(Disappearance of each mind moment noted)
|
Knowledge of Appearance as Terror
Knowledge of Contemplation of Danger
Dispassion
Desire for Deliverance
Contemplation of Reflexion
|
Discerning Formations as Void
|
Knowledge of Equanimity about Formations
(Abandonment of terror and delight)
|
Supramundane Path
(Experiences of Enlightenment)

Note: Path of Concentration reads across; path of Insight reads down.

Figure 1. The Buddhist Meditative Path According to the *Visuddhimagga*. Adapted from Nyanamoli, 1976, and Brown, 1986.

Complications

From the identification of the ego ideal and ideal ego with the concentration and insight practices, respectively, it is possible to describe the effects of meditation on narcissistic pathology and to understand some common psychological concomitants of meditative practices. The strengthening of the ego ideal by the concentration practices leads to a sense of cohesion, stability or serenity that can significantly relieve narcissistic anxieties of emptiness or isolation, producing a kind of "transitional object" to which an individual can turn for refuge. From a psychodynamic perspective, this is a major explanation of the many reports of positive psychotherapeutic effects of meditation in beginning practitioners. Yet if the ego ideal is strengthened without simultaneous insight into the nature of the ideal ego, the experience of the concentration practices may fuel an increasing sense of self-importance or specialness that can paradoxically strengthen the hold of the ideal ego. Individuals affected by such a dynamic may become self-righteous after tasting the fruits of meditation practice, believing themselves to be possessed of a special experience unattainable by those outside their circles. Others, especially those participating in religious groups centered around a charismatic leader, could become vulnerable to a kind of group merger with the idealized leader, who comes to personify the shared ego ideal, that can often lead to a suspension of critical judgment as the ego ideal becomes all important. "Basically, the identification with each other of the members of the small or large group permits them to experience a primitive narcissistic gratification of greatness and power" (Kernberg, 1984, p. 15) that often leads to a desire to act out that merger through unanticipated behavior, such as sexual relationships between teachers and group members, or violent acts aimed at non-believers.

When the ideal ego is investigated without sufficient support from the ego ideal, however, other effects occur. Without the stabilization of the concentration practices, those who undertake a too vigorous regime of the insight practices may become vulnerable to a range of fears, anxieties and inadequacies that can prove overwhelming to some. Those practitioners who become morbidly preoccupied with emptiness, show a lack of enthusiasm for living, and become overly serious about themselves and their spiritual calling probably represent a partially compensated attempt to deal with these anxieties. They suffer both from a forced and premature attempt to let go of belief in an abiding self, and from an inadequate ego ideal. Failing to experience union or the exaltation that such union engenders, and failing to satisfactorily project their image of perfection onto objects that can then stimulate their intrinsic capacities for love, they become overly serious, dry and rigidified. In most cases they succeed only in superimposing a new image of the ideal ego onto their preexisting one, this time cloaking the ideal ego in vestments of emptiness, egolessness and non-attachment. Yet the narcissistic attachment to such an image persists.

While these personality characteristics represent but the extremes of each imbalance, their descriptions can be instructive of the various ways in which narcissistic pathology can grow out of the meditative experience. The Buddhist texts are very clear about the need for precise balancing of concentration and insight practices, and, while they do not use the contemporary language of narcissism, it is clear that they are counseling an approach that balances an exalted, equilibrated, boundless state with one that stresses knowledge of the insubstantiality of the self. When these two experiences are not properly aligned, the jump into enlightenment is prohibited, and the attachment of the self to its own accomplishments remains possible. Meditation may ultimately be conceptualized as a vehicle for freeing an individual from his own narcissism, a liberation that is not complete until the experience of enlightenment. Until that point, the individual is subject to the pressures of his own narcissistic impulses, and the experiences of meditation may be recruited to satisfy those impulses, at the same time that those experiences force a confrontation with narcissistic attachments.

As has been shown, it is possible to trace the impact of the various meditative techniques on the psychic structures of narcissism, two of which, the ideal ego and ego ideal, have been outlined here. The relatively unfulfilled ego ideal, of which the individual may be vaguely aware in the form of yearnings to achieve a state of perfection, and the overly invested ideal ego, of which the individual is likely to be unaware, through the process of denial, are both accessed and transformed by the meditative path. Traditional Buddhist psychology lays great stress on the careful balancing of factors of concentration and insight, on experiences of terror and delight. This emphasis can also be interpreted, in the language of narcissism, to imply a need for the balancing of experiences of the ego ideal with those that confront the ideal ego. It is only when this balance is achieved that both may be abandoned and narcissism, itself, overcome.

To assert, therefore, that the meditative path can begin only when a cohesive self is attained is to run the risk of ignoring meditation's impact on the infantile narcissistic residue. To see meditation as usefully beginning only where Western personality theory leaves off may preclude an appreciation of how narcissism, itself, can be transformed by the experience of meditation. Eastern psychologies show us that growth need not stop at the so-called "mature" personalities, but in moving beyond these personalities, Eastern methods must confront narcissistic attachments that are recognized by both East and West, although described in different languages. Narcissism is rooted in the infantile state, persists in the adult, and inevitably interacts with the meditative experience. To understand this interaction is to recognize both the transformative power of meditation and the pervasive influence of narcissism.

References

Alexander, F. (1931). Buddhist training as an artificial catatonia. *Psychoanal. Rev., 18*, 129–45.

Andreas-Salome, L. (1962). The dual orientation of narcissism. *Psychoanal. Quarterly, 31*, 1–30.

Bonaparte, M. (1940). Time and the unconscious. *Int. J. Psycho-Anal., 21*, 427–63.

Brown, D. (1986). The states of meditation in cross-cultural perspective. In K. Wilber, J. Engler & D. Brown, *Transformations of consciousness.* Boston: New Science Library.

Chasseguet-Smirgel, J. (1975). *The ego ideal.* New York: W. W. Norton.

Engler, J. H. (1983). Vicissitudes of the self according to psychoanalysis and Buddhism: A spectrum model of object relations development. *Psychoanalysis and Contemporary Thought, 6:* 1, 29–72.

Engler, J. H. (1984). Therapeutic aims in psychotherapy and meditation: Developmental stages in the representation of self. *J. Transpersonal Psychol., 16:* 1, 25–62.

Epstein, M. & Lieff, J. (1981). Psychiatric complications of meditation practice. *J. Transpersonal Psychol., 13:* 2, 137–48.

Federn, P. (1952). *Ego psychology and the psychoses.* New York: Basic Books.

Freud, S. (1914). *On narcissism: An introduction. S.E., 14,* 67–102. London: Hogarth Press, 1957.

Freud, S. (1930). *Civilization and its discontents. S.E., 21,* 57–145. London: Hogarth Press, 1961.

Goleman, D. (1977). *The varieties of the meditative experience*. New York: Dutton.

Goleman, D. & Epstein, M. (1983). Meditation and well-being: An Eastern model of psychological health. In R. Walsh & D. Shapiro, *Beyond health and normality*. New York: Van Nostrand Reinhold.

Grunberger, B. (1971). *Narcissism*. New York: Int. Universities Press.

Guenther, H. V. (1974). *Philosophy and psychology in the Abhidharma*. Berkeley: Shambhala.

Guntrip, H. (1969). *Schizoid phenomena, object relations and the self*. New York: Basic Books.

Hanly, C. (1984). Ego ideal and ideal ego. *Int. J. Psycho-Anal., 65*, 253–61.

Jacobsen, E. (1964). *The self and the object world*. New York: Int. Universities Press.

Johansson, R. (1970). *The psychology of nirvana*. New York: Anchor.

Jones, E. (1913). The God complex. In: *Essays in applied psychoanalysis II*. London: Hogarth Press, 1951.

Jones, E. (1923). The nature of auto-suggestion. In *Papers on psychoanalysis*. Boston: Beacon Press, 1948.

Kernberg, O. (1975). *Borderline conditions and pathological narcissism*. New York: Aronson.

Kernberg, O. (1984). The couch at sea: Psychoanalytic studies of group and organizational leadership. *Int. J. Group Psychother., 34* (1), 5–23.

Kohut, H. (1966). Forms and transformations of narcissism. *J. Amer. Psychoanal. Assoc., 5*, 389–407.

Kohut, J. (1971). *The analysis of the self*. New York: Int. Universities Press.

Lewin, B. D. (1950). *The psychoanalysis of elation*. New York: W. W. Norton.

Mahler, M. (1972). On the first three subphases of the separation-individuation process. *Int. J. Psycho-Anal., 53*, 333–38.

Masson, J. (1974). India and the unconscious: Erik Erikson on Gandhi. *Int. J. Psycho-Anal., 55*, 519–29.

Masson, J. (1980). *The oceanic feeling: The origins of religious sentiment in Ancient India*. Dordrecht, Holland: D. Reidel.

Nyanamoli, B. (Transl.) (1976). *Visuddhimagga: The path of purification*, by Buddhaghosa, 2 vol. Boulder, CO: Shambhala.

Nyanaponika Thera (1962). *The heart of Buddhist meditation*. New York: S. Weiser.

Reich, A. (1960). Pathologic forms of self-esteem regulation. In: *Psychoanalytic contributions*. New York: Int. Universities Press, 1973.

Rose, G. (1972). Fusion states. In P. L. Giovacchini (Ed.), *Tactics and techniques in psychotherapy*. New York: Science House.

Ross, N. (1975). Affect as cognition: With observations on the meanings of
    mystical states. *Int. Rev. Psycho-Anal., 2,* 79–93.

Russell, E. (1986). Consciousness and the unconscious: Eastern meditative
    and Western psychotherapeutic approaches. *J. Transpersonal Psychol., 18*
    (1), 51–72.

Sandler, J., Holder, A., & Meers, D. (1963). The ego ideal and the ideal self.
    Psychoanal. Study of the Child, 18, 139–58.

Schroeder, T. (1922). Prenatal psychisms and mystical pantheism. *Int. J.
    Psycho-Anal. 3:* 4, 45–66.

Sun, Joe Tom (1924). Psychology in primitive Buddhism. *Psychoanal. Rev., 11,*
    39–47.

Wilber, K. (1980). The pre/trans fallacy. *ReVision,* 1980, *3,* 51–73.

Wilber, K. (1984a). The developmental spectrum and psychopathology:
    Part I. Stages and types of pathology. *J. Transpersonal Psychol., 16,* 75–118.

Wilber, K. (1984b). The developmental spectrum and psychopathology:
    Part II, Treatment modalities. *J. Transpersonal Psychol., 16,* 137–66.

II

The Deconstruction of the Self

Ego and "Egolessness" in Buddhist
Insight Meditation
(1988)

One of the casualties of the twentieth-century introduction of Eastern contemplative traditions to
the West has been the misappropriation of Freudian terminology by scholars and practitioners of
these Eastern traditions. Nowhere is this more evident than in
the confused use of the concepts "ego" and "egolessness" by
psychologists of the meditative experience (Engler, 1986, p. 18).
"Ego" has become variously equated with the rational mind,
the self-concept, or the experience of individuality and has
informally come to represent all that must be let go of in the
process of meditation. "Egolessness" has become an acceptable aspiration of those practicing meditation; yet, more often
than not, this goal is understood from a Western psychological perspective, rather than with the more subtle, originally

intended Eastern meaning. The word used in translation, "egolessness," has brought with it connotations of an upsurge in primary process thinking and id-dominated intrapsychic forces (Meissner, 1984, p. 229) that are often mistakenly embraced by Western practitioners eager to jettison their egos. As a result, concepts that include the Buddhist "anatman" (no-self) doctrine and the psychodynamic "ego" are often understood only superficially, hampering dialogue and understanding between the two traditions.

The Fate of the Ego

The fate of the ego in Buddhist meditation, in fact, has not been clearly delineated in Western psychological terms. The tendency of contemporary theorists has been to propose developmental schema in which meditation systems develop "beyond the ego" (Walsh & Vaughan, 1980), yet this approach has ignored aspects of the ego which are not abandoned and which are, in fact, developed through meditation practice itself. Familiarity with the current ego psychological-object relations view of the ego reveals that meditation can be seen as operating in different ways on many distinctive facets of the ego, promoting change and development *within* the ego, rather than beyond it. This view requires that the ego be understood as a complex and sophisticated matrix of structures, functions and representations, rather than as a single entity that could be readily abandoned. It recognizes the indispensability of the ego while at the same time revealing how meditation practice can uniquely modify it, producing an ego no longer obsessed with its own solidity.

Buddhist meditation systems that stress the development of mindfulness and the cultivation of insight (vipassana) specifically focus on the "experience of I" within the meditation. The "I" which is investigated is that which is felt to be "permanent, unitary, and under its own power" (Gyatso, 1984, p. 162) or which seems to be a "substantially existent or self-sufficient entity" (ibid.). It is the "independent I under its own power" (ibid., p. 163) that is revealed through meditation to be lacking in "inherent existence" (Hopkins, 1984, p. 141) and "merely designated in dependence upon the aggregates of mind and body" (Gyatso, 1984, p. 163). Thus, in accordance with a modern object relations view of the self-concept as a "fused and confused . . . constantly changing series of self-images" (Jacobsen, 1964, p. 20), the "I" experience is revealed to be a constantly changing impersonal process, increasingly insubstantial the more carefully it is examined. As a result, the self-concept that was once experienced as solid, cohesive and real (see Guenther, 1974, p. 139) becomes increasingly differentiated, fragmented, elusive and ultimately transparent. This is the cardinal concept of "anatta,"[1] "the idea of persisting individual nature" (ibid., p. 207) that is destroyed through meditative insight.

It is this realization that is at the core of what has conventionally become known as "egolessness," and it is clear that such an understanding is not one that is easily reconciled with Western psychoanalytic notions of the personality (Goleman & Epstein, 1983). Yet to conceive of this understanding as equivalent to "moving beyond" the ego is to ignore much of what years of exploration of the ego have revealed. This exploration has mapped the structure and functions of the ego sufficiently that the changes in the "experience of I" enumerated within the Theravadin Buddhist system can, in fact, be explained within the psychoanalytic framework of the ego.

The System Ego

As can be seen from Figure 2, psychoanalytic understanding of the ego has fleshed out much of Freud's original formulations. The ego is now understood in representational (Rothstein, 1981) as well as functional terms, with the former stressing the process by which a picture of the self and world is built up out of multiple mental images, constructs or "representations," and the latter stressing the various roles or functions that the ego plays within the psychic economy in maintaining psychic equilibrium and facilitating adaptation and growth. Ego functions are thus to be distinguished from the "self" and the "self-representation" (Stolorow, 1975, p. 180), and the ego is seen as a system composed of structures and sub-structures which can be in collaboration or conflict (Hartmann, 1950, 1958). Rothstein (1981) integrated this formulation with those of post-Freudian elaborators of object relations theory by conceptualizing "the representational world as a substructure of the ego of equal importance to the substructure of ego functions and importantly related to them" (Rothstein, 1981, p. 440).

Thus, the often referred to notion of Freud's (1923) that the ego is that which "masters the tensions," "controls instincts," "regulates the drives" or "postpones and controls the discharges of excitations into the external world" becomes but one of the substructures of ego function. This is the classic view of the ego as supervisor of "all its own constituent processes" (ibid.) or as mediator between demands of id and super-ego or id and environment. Other important functions, elaborated soon thereafter, include those of defense or inhibition (A. Freud, 1937), adaptation or reality mastery (Hartmann, 1950, 1958), and, most significantly for this discussion, that of synthesis.

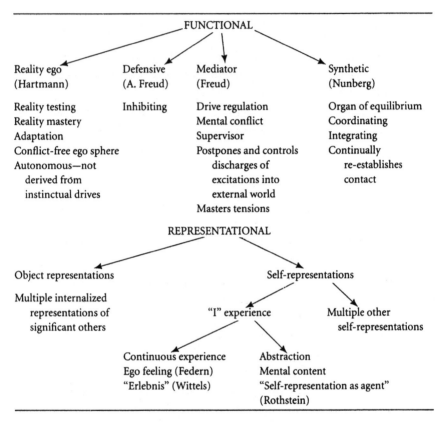

Figure 2. System Ego

This synthetic function acts as an "organ of equilibrium" within the internal world, promoting integration and organization of diverse and conflicting inputs and components (Nunberg, 1955). As Freud, himself, made clear, it is opposed to the function of repression (Freud, 1923), which splits off and isolates conflicted material from awareness. Its role is to assimilate the products of an ever-fluctuating and increasingly differentiated psyche, without rejection, facilitating a stable and

coherent (Nunberg, 1955, p. 153) experience. "The ego medi-
ates, unifies, integrates because it is of its essence to maintain,
on more and more complex levels of differentiation and objectivation of reality, the original unity" (Loewald, 1951, p. 14).

The representational component of the ego comple-
ments the functional view by stressing the "conglomerate of
pre-individuated impressions" (Rothstein, 1981, p. 440) that
pattern into mental images of the self. It is through the development of the representational dimension that the individual's coherent self-experience is built up, contributing to the
creation of a sense of a solid "I." The means by which this
occurs has been the subject of debate within analytic circles for
years, with some asserting that the "I" is experienced affec-
tively (viscerally) and other cognitively (as an abstraction).
Federn, for example, spoke of "ego feeling" as the "sensation,
constantly present, of one's own person" (Federn, 1952, p. 60)
and insisted that it was a "continuous experience" rather than
a "conceptual abstraction" (p. 283). Wittels (1949) also spoke
of the ego as "a direct inner experience" (p. 54) and, by attach-
ing the Germanic concept of "Erlebnis," tried to connote the
inner reverberations of being that are interpreted as "I." While
not rejecting the role of the affective experience, Rothstein
(1981) also emphasized the manner in which "I" may become
a belief or abstraction. From an abstract perspective, Rothstein conceptualized the "I" experience as a content of the
ego, which he designated as "the self-representation as agent"
(ibid., p. 440).

Thus, the "I" is not identical with the ego but is more
precisely a component. It is described as a self-representation
as agent because it sees itself as the *one* capable of activity. It
"conceives of itself as existing actively to pursue and insure
its well-being and survival" (ibid., p. 440). It is an idea, an

abstraction, contained within the ego, that embodies the ego's sense of itself as solid and real. It is not, however, to be confused with the entire ego. Developed out of the ego's continuing sensation of itself, it remains, nevertheless, at base a concept that the person holds dear.

At the core of the self-representation as agent lies the narcissistically invested ideal ego (Epstein, 1986), "an idea which the ego has of itself" as perfect and inviolable (Hanly, 1984). The ideal ego involves a sense of *inherent* perfection, a "state of being" equivalent to the Tibetan description of the "independent I *under its own power.*" It is an ideal that is not recognized as such, but is, instead, deeply felt to be real, denying all transience, insignificance and mortality.

Effects of Insight

Meditation systems, then, that develop the factors of mindfulness and insight focus particularly on the "ego feeling" of an "independent I." While concentration practices can temporarily suspend ego boundaries and provide a deep sense of ontological security through the merger of ego and ego ideal (Epstein, 1986), insight practices operate within the ego system itself. Attending both to the subjective intimation of the experiencing I *and* to the abstract cognitions that form it on a conceptual level, insight practices seek to uncover the elementary particles of the "I" experience. This occurs through a definite sequence of events that profoundly alters the structure of the ego.

As meditation develops, the various self-representations first come into and out of focus. These include those that have served as "the repository and container of various fears concerning oneself" (Joseph, 1987, p. 14) and those which have become "narcissistically and/or masochistically invested" (Rothstein, 1981, p. 441). Exposure of these representations through the non-judgmental light of mindfulness permits a simultaneous dis-identification from and integration of self-images that have often been unquestioned assumptions or split off rejections. As meditation deepens, the representational nature of the grosser self-concepts becomes clear, but a more subtle and pervasive tendency to identify with experience persists. This tendency to identify surfaces most often as a resistance to mindfulness ["This is mine, this is I, this is my self" (Nyanamoli, 1976, p. 743)] and is attended to just as are resistances in psychoanalysis which mask unconscious material. In this manner, the "experience of I" is ultimately deconstructed (Engler, 1983) in terms synonymous with what is implied by the self-representation as agent, as an image, abstraction or simulacrum. The ability of the ideal ego to "influence the ego's self-observing activities even to the extent of causing the ego to deny its own nature" (Hanly, 1984, p. 260) is finally extinguished. The self is not eliminated; it is revealed to be what it has always been. "Selflessness is not a case of something that existed in the past becoming non-existent; rather, this sort of 'self' is something that never did exist. What is needed is to identify as non-existent something that always was non-existent . . ." (Gyatso, 1984, p. 40).

What is unusual about the Buddhist view from an object relations perspective is the assertion that an individual could experience the pure representational process without becoming destabilized. Thus, while the uncovering of the self-representation as agent is one major modification of the ego system produced by insight meditation, it is unlikely to be the only one. From the representational point of view this is clearly the major transformation. Yet from a functional perspective, a further compensatory modification is required in order for the requisite stability to be conferred, stability that could only derive from the synthetic capacity of the ego.

The development of mindfulness, like that of evenly suspended attention (Epstein, 1984), involves a "therapeutic split in the ego" (Engler, 1983, p. 48; Sterba, 1934), in which the ego becomes both subject and object, observer and observed. This capacity for observing the dynamic flow of psychic events is very much a synthetic function, maintaining equilibrium in the face of incessant change. Just as the synthetic function of the ego is said to hold objective reality to itself, "detached from itself, before it, not in it" (Loewald, 1951, p. 18), so does mindfulness, in the traditional Buddhist psychological text, "guard and confront an objective field," "steadying the object" and "keeping it immoveable" (Nyanamoli, 1976, p. 524). Mindfulness maintains a sense of connection within mind moments whose transience becomes increasingly evident as meditation progresses. "It should be regarded as like a pillar because it is firmly founded, or as like a door-keeper" (ibid., p. 524) because of the way in which it guards the mind and sense-doors in the face of change. Mindfulness allows each moment to be experienced in its entirety; it is synthetic because it binds awareness to the object, neither holding on to, nor rejecting, whatever projects itself in the mind.

This synthetic function of mindfulness recalls what one of Freud's teachers (Pierre Janet, in 1903) referred to as the pinnacle of healthy mental functioning, the "synthetic operation" of attention to "the formation in the mind of the present moment" that he termed "pre-sentification," "the capacity for grasping reality to the maximum" (Ellenberger, 1970, p. 376). Janet understood that this capacity could be developed and that to do so contributed to the sense of psychological well-being. "The natural tendency of the mind is to roam through the past and the future; it requires a certain effort to keep one's attention in the present, and still more to concentrate it on present action. 'The real present for us is an act of a certain complexity which we grasp as one single state of consciousness in spite of this complexity, and in spite of its real duration. . . . Pre-sentification consists of making present a state of mind and a group of phenomena'" (ibid.).

Advanced stages of insight meditation involve profound experiences of dissolution and fragmentation, yet the practitioner, through the practice of "making present," is able to withstand these psychic pressures. It is the ego, primarily through its synthetic function, that permits integration of the experience of disintegration. In true egolessness, there could be only disintegration, and such a state would manifest as psychosis. The ego system is certainly a target of these meditation practices, but what results is more properly conceived of as an intrasystemic (Hartmann, 1958; Rothstein, 1981) reequilibration rather than a progression beyond an outmoded structure.

As the moment-to-moment nature of reality becomes more and more directly experienced, it is the synthetic function of the ego, as mindfulness, that must continuously re-establish contact with the object of awareness. "To maintain, or constantly re-establish, this unity . . . by integrating and synthesizing what seems to move further and further away from it and fall into more and more unconnected parts" (Loewald, 1951, p. 14) remains a function of the ego that is *not* obliterated through meditation but that becomes increasingly necessary as the self-representation as agent loses its authority. Through this relentless exposure, insight meditation radically alters the experience of the representational world. What once seemed solid is now perceived at its quantum level, more differentiated and patterned, more highly complex and fragmentary, more disconnected, and less coherent, real and inherently existent. As the representational aspect of the ego is decathected, there is a compensatory evolution of the functional component, such that the higher order of differentiation can be integrated. "Conscious reflection," argues Loewald (1978), is necessary for the *development* of the ego, for the attainment of a "higher organization of psychic processes" (Joseph, 1987). The Buddhists texts agree. Mindfulness, the vehicle of conscious reflection, of "remembering and not forgetting" (Nyanamoli, 1976, p. 524), leads to insight into the differentiated nature of the psyche and propels the development of the synthetic aspect of the ego, preserving, on a moment-to-moment basis, the integrity of a more highly complex psyche.

Thus, mindfulness is not a means of forgetting the ego; it is a method of using the ego to observe its own manifestations. Development of the capacity to attend to the moment-to-moment nature of the mind allows the representational nature of the self to be experienced without the distortions of idealization, thereby promoting a change within the ego system different from that envisioned by most Western personality theory. Rather than encouraging a consolidated ego sure of its own solidity, the Buddhist approach envisions a more fluid ego able to constantly integrate potentially destabilizing experiences of insubstantiality and impermanence. From this perspective the great promise of the Buddhist psychologies can be fully appreciated. The enlightened ego abides, but in a form which sustains the realization of impersonality. As the Dalai Lama has expressed it, "This seemingly solid, concrete, independent, self-instituting I under its own power that appears actually does not exist at all" (Gyatso, 1984, p. 70).

Note

1. "Anatta" means no "atta" or no self.

References

Ellenberger, H. (1970). *The discovery of the unconscious.* New York: Basic Books.

Engler, J. (1983). Vicissitudes of the self according to psychoanalysis and Buddhism: A spectrum model of object relations development. *Psychoanalysis and Contemporary Thought, 6:* 1, 29–72.

Engler, J. (1986). Therapeutic aims in psychotherapy and meditation. In K. Wilber, J. Engler, & D. P. Brown, *Transformations of consciousness.* Boston: New Science Library.

Epstein, M. (1984). On the neglect of evenly suspended attention. *Journal of Transpersonal Psycho., 16,* 2, 193–205.

Epstein, M. (1986). Meditative transformations of narcissism. *Journal of Transpersonal Psychol., 18,* 2, 143–158.

Federn, P. (1952). *Ego psychology and the psychoses.* New York: Basic Books.

Freud, A. (1937). *The ego and the mechanisms of defense.* New York: Int. Univ. Press.

Freud, S. (1923). *The ego and the id.* New York: Norton.

Freud, S. (1926). The question of lay analysis. S.E. XX, London: Hogarth Press, 1955, 179–258.

Goleman, D. & Epstein, M. (1983). Meditation and well-being: An Eastern model of psychological health. In R. Walsh and D. H. Shapiro, *Beyond health and normality.* New York: Van Nostrand Reinhold.

Guenther, H. V. (1974). *Philosophy and psychology in the Abhidharma.* Berkeley: Shambhala.

Gyatso, T. (1984). *Kindness, clarity, and insight.* Ithaca: Snow Lion.

Hanly, C. (1984). Ego ideal and ideal ego. *Int. J. Psycho-Anal., 65:* 253–61.

Hartmann, H. (1950). Comments on the psychoanalytic theory of the ego. *Psychoanal. Study of the Child, 5:* 74–96.

Hartmann, H. (1958). *Ego psychology and the problem of adaptation.* New York: Int. Univ. Press.

Hopkins, J. (1984). *The tantric distinction.* London: Wisdom Publications.

Jacobsen, E. (1964). *The self and the object world.* New York: Int. Univ. Press.

Joseph. E. J. (1987). The consciousness of being conscious. *J. Am. Psychoanal. Assoc., 35:* 1, 5–22.

Loewald, H. W. (1951). Ego and reality. *Int. J. Psycho-Anal. 32:* 10–18.

Loewald, H. W. (1978). Instinct theory, object relations, and psychic structure formation. *J. Amer. Psychoanal. Assn.*, 26: 453–506.

Meissner, W. W. (1984). *Psychoanalysis and religious experience.* New Haven:
Yale University Press.

Nunberg, H. (1955). *Principles of psychoanalysis.* New York: Int. Univ. Press.

Nyanamoli, B. (Transl.) (1976). *Visuddhimagga: The path of purification,* by
Buddhaghosa, 2 vol. Boulder: Shambhala.

Rothstein, A. (1981). The ego: An evolving construct. *Int. J. Psycho-Anal.* 62:
435–45.

Sterba, R. F. (1934). *The fate of the ego in analytic therapy. Int. J. Psycho-Anal.*
15: 117–126.

Stolorow, R. D. (1975). Toward a functional definition of narcissism. *Int. J.
Psycho-Anal.,* 56: 179–185.

Walsh, R. H. & Vaughan, F. (1980). *Beyond ego.* Los Angeles: Tarcher.

Wittels, F. (1949). A neglected boundary of psychoanalysis. *Psychoanal.
Quart.,* 18: 44–59.

III

Forms of Emptiness

Psychodynamic, Meditative and
Clinical Perspectives
(1989)

I n my efforts to synthesize Buddhist and psychodynamic psychologies of mind, the inner experience of emptiness has emerged as the most beguiling and yet the most treacherous subject common to both fields. There is confusion within psychodynamic theory about what constitutes emptiness, there is confusion within Buddhist theory about what constitutes emptiness, and there is certainly confusion among psychodynamic psychotherapists about what Buddhists mean by emptiness, and confusion among Buddhists about what psychotherapists mean by emptiness. The word is applied to such an array of states of mind that its meaning has become virtually impossible to grasp. Yet a careful examination of the various forms of emptiness does much to illuminate the special contribution of Buddhist thought to contemporary understanding of the nature of the self.

Too Marvelous to Comprehend

Experientially, emptiness has been invoked to explain almost every possible alteration in the experience of self. Thus, it can refer to the confusing numbness of the psychotic, the "despairing incompleteness" (Singer, 1979) of the personality disorders, the depersonalized state in which one aspect of the self is repudiated while the observing ego becomes hyperaware (Levy, 1984), identity diffusion, in which the self seeps out and fuses with whatever surrounds it, existential meaninglessness and Buddhist ultimate reality. The word used to describe these states is the same, but the experiences are all quite different.

While the emptiness that grows out of Buddhist meditation can be difficult to describe, it is often seen as holding great promise for those afflicted with the more pathological emptinesses described above. At times attributed to Mind, in its larger sense, and at times to the self, the experience is said to be "intangible," "like a mute person tasting sugar" (Kalu Rinpoche, 1986, p. 111). At other times adjectives like "clear, open, and unimpeded" (Kalu, 1986, p. 33) are used to convey its sense. "There is just the omni-present voidness of the real self-existent Nature of everything, and no more" (Blofeld, 1958, p. 50), said Huang Po, a ninth-century Chinese Zen teacher. "All these phenomena are intrinsically void and yet this Mind with which they are identical is no mere nothingness. By this I mean that it does exist, but in a way too marvellous for us to comprehend. It is an existence which is no existence, a non-existence which is nevertheless existence" (Blofeld, 1958, p. 108).

The Tibetan Mahamudra texts describe several possible experiences of emptiness:

> Some may feel that all things become empty, or may see the void nature of the world; others experience all things as devoid of self-entity, or that both body and mind are non-existent; while yet others really understand the truth of Voidness (Sunyata). (Chang, 1963, p. 41)

How can we understand this? Let us first return to ostensibly firmer ground.

Psychological Emptiness

From a structural perspective, in terms of the "postulated unconscious psychic organizations" (Lichtenberg, 1975, p. 45) that are so essential to psychodynamic thought, emptiness has been explained in the following ways: 1) as a deficiency, 2) as a defense, 3) as a defect in self/object integration, and 4) as the result of inner conflict over idealized aspirations of the self (Singer, 1977a; Levy, 1984). Let us look at each.

The deficiency model posits emptiness as the internalized remnant of "emotional sustenance" not given (Singer, 1977a, p. 461). Whether it be from "loss, rejection, unavailability or ambivalence" (p. 461) the essential point is, in the words of Winnicott, to "think not of trauma but of nothing happening when something might profitably have happened" (Winnicott, 1974, p. 106). The narcissistic parent who treats the child as if he or she does not exist (Giovacchini, 1972, p. 377) or the "deserting but desireable" (Guntrip, 1971) parent sets up in the child a condition in which "object representations" and "outer world" manifestations are excessively clung to while deficient attachment develops to self-representations. Those self-representations that do emerge are colored by the "split-off negative value" of the unavailable object (Singer, 1977a, p. 462). What results is an "emptying of the self" with concordant fears of being swallowed, extinguished, imprisoned, absorbed or lost in a "vacuum of experience" (Guntrip, 1971, p. 291).

The defense model sees emptiness as a more tolerable substitution for virulent rage or self-hatred (Giovacchini, 1972), a "defense against recognition by the hidden critical agencies of the actual presence of the (so-called) bad mother" (Singer, 1977a, p. 468). While at first this emptiness may in some sense seem preferable to the direct experience of that against which it is defending, the resulting fear of emptiness can become virtually intolerable. Thus, this fear can begin to represent "the evil, tantalizing and unspeakable torturing potential of the uncontrolled, unencapsulated, freed, bad and empty object starving, like the self, within" (Singer, 1977b, p. 478).

The defect model sees disturbances in the development of the sense of self, an inability to harmoniously integrate diverse and conflicting "component groups" of self and object representations, as the underlying mechanism behind the experience of emptiness (Singer, 1977b, p. 472). Here, the lack of a cohesive self, a failure to navigate Mahler's rapprochement subphase of infantile development such that good and bad impressions can be tolerated with regard to the same object, predisposes to feelings of emptiness. Emptiness here is seen as the "loss of the normal background feeling tone guaranteed by cohesiveness of internalized object relations" (Levy, 1984, p. 393) or as the result of opposing ego identifications in which one part of the ego is "repudiated or eliminated as being dead or unreal and is observed by the intact part of the ego" (Levy, 1984, p. 392).

Traditionally, there are said to be three component groups of self-images that must be blended and balanced (Singer, 1977b, p. 472) in order to protect against this kind of emptiness. They are (1) "self-images based on body experiences associated with instinctual need gratification" (Lichtenberg, 1975, p. 461), the so-called "body-self," (2) "self-images that emerge as entities having discrete differentiation from objects" (Lichtenberg, 1975, p. 461), the result of separation/individuation and the un-coupling of all-good and all-bad self/object representations, and (3) "self-images that, by virtue of idealization retain a sense of grandiosity and omnipotence shared with an idealized object" (Lichtenberg, 1975, p. 461). These latter self-images derive from "archaic fantasies" that originate in early life in the state of primary narcissism or "total mother-infant merging" (Lichtenberg, 1975, p. 461) and which are of two types: (a) grandiose, omnipotent images of the self, the so-called "ideal ego" (Hanly, 1984), and (b) idealized images of the parents which have both self and object qualities (Lichtenberg, 1975, p. 464), the so-called "ego-ideal" (Hanly, 1984).

The fourth model, that of conflicts over idealized aspirations, is really a subset of the third, with particular emphasis on the idealized self-images. In these cases, emptiness is felt when internalized, unconscious, idealized images of the self are not matched by actual experience, producing a sense of unreality or "estrangement" (Federn, 1952, p. 61). There is a kind of disavowal here of the actual self, or the actual experience, under pressure from the ideal ego, which has become, in essence, a functional aspect of the super-ego (Hanly, 1984). With this disavowal, this inability to "measure up" to the internalized standards of unconscious fundamental beliefs, comes a sense of emptiness. Because we retain a grandiose image of ourselves, rooted in archaic fantasy, as solid, deep, firm and, in some sense, immortal, when our actual experience does not correspond, we cannot relinquish the idealized image, but we are stuck—confused—we experience a loss of meaning, a sense of emptiness, that suddenly seems very real.

Let us now return to the Buddhist view of emptiness, to some more precise definitions of just what this experience represents in order to see whether it has any relevance for what has already been described.

Buddhist Emptiness

According to the Buddhist scholar Herbert Guenther (1974), "sunyata," or emptiness, is the experience which "serves to destroy the idea of a persisting individual nature" (p. 207). It is not an end in itself, but is only meant to "crush the belief in concrete existence." This is a crucial point, emphasized also by the thirteenth-century Japanese Zen master, Dogen. "Originally," he said, "the various 'emptinesses' were needed to break through existence. But once/since there are no existents, what 'emptiness' is needed?" (Cleary, 1986, p. 19). The contrast with the aforementioned Western experiences of emptiness is immediate; emptiness is not something real in itself, not a "vacuity of nothingness" (Hopkins, 1987, p. 200), or an "annihilation of everything" (p. 44), but a *specific* negative of inherent existence. As Nagarjuna wrote, "Emptiness has been said . . . to be the relinquishment of views, but . . . those who hold to the view of emptiness are incurable" (Cleary, 1986, p. 19).

More specifically, emptiness is said to be the "non-affirming negative of the inherently existent I" (Hopkins, 1987). As described most particularly in the texts of the Gelukpa school of Tibetan Buddhism and detailed most recently by Jeffrey Hopkins (1987) in a treatise entitled *Emptiness Yoga,* emptiness assumes a central function in explicating the Buddhist notions of the nature of the self. The Gelukpas hold that one must use the intellect to prepare the ground for meditative insight, that there must be an element of "valid cognition" (p. 41) in perceptions for meditative understanding to unfold. Without this, there is the danger of going nowhere in meditation, of using techniques to verify a deluded perspective. This school is very careful to lay out an exhaustively analyzed conceptual model of emptiness whose basic tenets hold for most of the other schools. Kalu Rinpoche, a teacher of the Kagyu school known for its emphasis on practice and direct experience, nevertheless affirms, "It is said that someone who tries to meditate without a conceptual understanding of what he or she is doing is like a blind person trying to find the way in open country: such a person can only wander about, with no idea how to choose one direction over another" (Kalu Rinpoche, 1986, p. 113).

The first step in understanding emptiness is to focus on the "inherently existent I," to actually find it as it appears. It is a belief, a "false estimation of the nature of oneself" (Kalu, 1986, p. 37), an innate misperception, a "falsely conceived" (Hopkins, 1987, p. 56) image of the self that nevertheless appears to us as real. We must find it in our own experience.

So the first step is to have an actual sense of concrete existence, to "ascertain well the appearance of a substantially existent I" (p. 65), to have a "clear feeling of the object to be negated" (Kalu, 1986, p. 83). Without this, it is like "dispatching the troops with no sense of the enemy" (Hopkins, 1987,

p. 47). This conception can, in the Buddhist view, be quite subtle and deep-seated. In passages that are unusual because of their implications of a dynamic unconscious, these texts assert that "subliminal consciousnesses" (p. 133) passively and continuously accept the reality of a substantially existent I. The point is not to withdraw the mind in meditative absorption from the "coarser conceptions of the self" (p. 120). This is said to be like "reforming a naughty child by removing it from sight." The usual mind that is convinced that a truly established person exists must be relentlessly identified. It is only through this identification that emptiness reveals itself, for the "inherently existent I" turns out to be "analytically unfindable and only nominally imputed" (p. 105); in meditative stabilization emptiness appears only as "an *absence* of the object it qualifies" (p. 61). "A strong sense of being unable to find what you were formerly sure could be found" (p. 200) comes into being and, in a stage of meditation termed "inferential cognition of emptiness," the object disappears and only an *image*, a conceptual consciousness, of the negative, or absence, of inherent existence remains.

So emptiness is a finding of the "nonabsoluteness" (Cleary, 1986, p. 36) of things, of their indefinability. It does not mean that they do not exist *at all*, but that they have no *inherent* existence. Emptiness does not challenge the validity of the "conceptually designated dimension of . . . relative phenomena" (Namgyal, 1986, p. xxxiv), of the "conventionally existent I" (Hopkins, 1987, p. 112), but only of its conceived object, the inherently existent I. "The I is not just an illusory figment of the imagination like a rope-snake, but an existent phenomenon; however, we do not know it as it is, qualified by *mere* existence" (Hopkins, 1987, p. 149). So the finding of emptiness strips the I of the habitual misconceptions that permeate our usual experience of ourselves.

The final point is that emptiness is a *non-affirming* negative. Non-affirming means that something positive is not being substituted for the object of negation. Emptiness is always found *in relation to* a belief in an object's inherent existence. It is not a "vacuity of nothingness" (Hopkins, 1987) that has a reality of its own; it is an understanding that the concrete appearances to which we are accustomed do not exist in the way we imagine (p. 200).

With regard to the sense of self, the point is not that some firmly established self is abandoned for a greater "egolessness," but that, in the words of the present Dalai Lama, "this seemingly solid, concrete, independent, self-instituting I under its own power that appears actually does not exist at all" (Gyatso, 1984, p. 70). The understanding of one who has realized emptiness has thus been compared to a person's knowledge that he is wearing sunglasses. "The very appearance of the distorted color induces knowledge that it is not true" (Gyatso, 1984, p. 80).

From a psychodynamic perspective, there is a rather remarkable parallel between the Buddhist view of a subliminal tendency to see the I as inherently existent and the psychoanalytic notion of an unconscious "ideal ego" that conceives of itself as perfect, permanent and immortal, as "vouchsafed a state of perfection" (Hanly, 1984). It is this ideal ego, derived, as we have seen, from the grandiosity of primary narcissism, that is responsible, from a metapsychological perspective, for denying the ego's true nature (Epstein, 1986). Compare this ideal ego with the Buddhist definition of the "self of personality" that is exposed by the realization of emptiness. "(It) consists of the innate consciousness that assigns to itself, as its own nature, an eternal, independent entity and thereby clings to the notion of 'I' or 'self' " (Namgyal, 1986, p. 55).

The emptiness of the Buddhist practices, then, is in some ways the converse of the emptiness that is produced by conflict over idealized self-images, and this is why, I believe, it speaks to that emptiness in some intuitive way. Rather than succumbing to the inevitable gap between actual and idealized experience of the self by disavowing the actual self through a numbing sense of hollowness or unreality, the Buddhist approach seeks to uncover the distorting idealizations which are at their root groundless, based on archaic infantile fantasy. So meditators troubled by a sense of emptiness must not mistake this for Buddhist emptiness; they must go inside it, investigate it, expose their beliefs in *its* concrete nature, just as they must do for their more elusive, but not necessarily less tenacious, ideal egos. The result is not an attachment to emptiness as a thing in itself, not an identification with emptiness of the sort that characterizes *all* of the pathological forms of emptiness described above, but a mere absence or negation of belief in a persisting individual nature.

Throughout the Buddhist tradition it is recognized that even this understanding of emptiness is precarious, that it, too, can be distorted by the need to identify *something* as existing in its own right. In the words of the 4th Zen Patriarch,

> The practice of bodhisattvas has emptiness as its realization: when beginning students see emptiness, this is seeing emptiness, it is not real emptiness. Those who cultivate the Way and attain real emptiness do not see emptiness or nonemptiness; *they* have no views. (Cleary, 1986, p. 19)

Pitfalls

Those personality types prone to pathological emptiness who begin Buddhist meditation practices designed to uncover Buddhist emptiness face several potential pitfalls. In the borderline personality, for instance, what is most lacking is the synthetic or integrative capacity of the ego to consolidate and maintain multiple, conflicting self/object representations. The relationship of the self with internalized object relationships is distorted by the defense of splitting, in which all good and all bad representations of the same person cannot be integrated. Similarly, splitting can persist between the grandiose, idealized self/object and the "deflated, debased" self/object (Lichtenberg, 1975), and the ideal ego may remain fused with primitive all-good object representations, rather than separating off into the superego. The mindfulness practices actually strengthen the synthetic capacities of the ego (Epstein, 1988) by training the observing ego to attend to whatever arises without clinging or condemnation, thus allowing conflicting images to present themselves just as they are. So mindfulness practices can actually be very helpful in decreasing the pathologized emptiness of the borderline personality. *However,* if the insight practices into the emptiness of the ideal ego are attempted prematurely, there are real risks of the loss of the good self-images with which it may be fused, with the preservation and exacerbation of the all-bad, destructive images provoking the borderline's characteristic defensive flight into depersonalization or identity loss. This would undoubtedly be absolutely terrifying, and this kind of scenario is not uncommon among populations of Western students who undertake intensive practice.

The narcissistic personality is a different story. According to Kernberg's (1982) formulation for severe narcissistic disturbances, between the ages of 3 and 5, all of the positive representations of self and objects are put together along with the idealized representations into a structure that he terms the pathological grandiose self. All of the negative aspects are projected onto others and aggression is expressed as devaluation of others. Ideal ego representations are incorporated into this pathological grandiose self, leaving only the "aggressively determined components," which tend to be dissociated and projected, in the superego (p. 134). Emptiness in the narcissist is a result of the void that is created in the internal world of object relations through the constant devaluation of others (Kernberg, 1982). This is a pervasive feeling that can be temporarily interrupted only by admiration from others (Kernberg, 1975), which tends to be all that is sought in intimate relationships. It is extremely difficult for the narcissistic personality to uncover the sense of inherent existence embodied in the ideal ego because of its fusion in the pathological grandiose self. Narcissists are much more likely to subvert the notion of "non-self" or "egolessness," incorporating that image back into their ideal egos, becoming arrogant about their special understanding and using Buddhist veneration of emptiness as justification for their paucity of meaningful relationships.

The schizoid personality tends to feel emptiness as an "innate quality" (Kernberg, 1975) of their being that makes them different from other people, who they can see have feelings of "love, hatred, tenderness, longing or mourning" (p. 215) that they find unavailable within themselves. The schizoid stance has been seen as a defense against feeling longing for "emotional supplies from a good object" (Stewart, 1985) or as the result of "destructive impulses turned from the object towards his own ego" (Klein, 1946, p. 19). In either case, these people feel disintegrated, rather than anxious, unable to experience emotion, unable to contact others, and most in touch with a "soothing" (Kernberg, 1975), "amorphous experience of indefiniteness and weakness" (Guntrip, 1971, p. 97). Successful meditation for them involves a gradual process whereby contact is first made with the ego ideal through the concentration practices, providing a sense of ontological security to counter their pervasive insecurity and allowing the soothing emptiness to be gradually relinquished. At this point the mindfulness practices can begin to uncover the emotional traces that have been unattended to. The obvious mis-use of meditation here is as a validation and reinforcement of the schizoid view of "no feelings" as an absolute truth. The Zen chant of "No eyes, no ears, no mouth, etc." can readily serve as a schizoid defense when incorrectly apprehended.

In the depressive personality, emptiness functions as a kind of one step beyond loneliness. Not only is the loved object missed and longed for, but there is an internal void and a feeling of an incapacity for love. There may be a deeply felt sense of unworthiness that attributes the loss of the other to the person's own badness (Kernberg, 1975); thus depressed persons come to feel that they do not deserve to be loved or appreciated. The therapeutic value of meditation for these people lies in the establishment of contact with a valued internal object through the concentration practices that release feelings of love, joy, contentment, and oneness. This is not a substitute for establishing intimate relationships, but it does reveal to depressed personalities that they are capable of feeling what they thought themselves incapable of.

The major psychological issue for those with conflicts over their idealized self-images is often a kind of shame, or unworthiness, that arises when the discrepancy between actual and idealized self is too great (Singer, 1977a, p. 463). This unworthiness can block access to good internal self/objects, creating a sense of being "cut off" from love, of incompleteness. Without a working through of this incompleteness, which can be facilitated both by meditation and by psychotherapy, the pre-existing sense of emptiness may never be fully abandoned. There is a real danger, in these personalities, of never progressing beyond the concentration practices, of resting in a state where the sense of unworthiness is being off-set but where the fundamental misconceptions of an inherent self are not examined.

This is also the fundamental danger for the rest of us in progressing on the path of meditation. We are all prone to ignore the falsely conceived self by dwelling in the tranquil stabilization that meditation practice offers. These states, which can become ineffably sublime, offer experiences of oneness far removed from our usual personalities that can be mistaken for emptiness by an untrained practitioner. Yet the ultimate purpose of Buddhist meditation is not to withdraw from the falsely conceived self but to *recognize* the misconception, thereby weakening its influence. "Without disbelieving the object of this (misconception)," said Dharmakirti, "it is impossible to abandon (misconceiving it)" (Hopkins, 1987, p. 137). There is a deep, tenacious resistance to this disbelief, a kind of clutching that occurs, a fear of an emptiness that is conceived to be as real as the inherently existent I. In the words of Huang Po, "Men are afraid to forget their minds, fearing to fall through the Void with nothing to stay their fall. They do not know that the Void is not really void, but the realm of the real Dharma" (Blofeld, 1958, p. 41).

References

Blofeld, J. (1958). *The Zen teaching of Huang Po.* New York: Grove Press.

Chang, G. C. C. (1963). *Teachings of Tibetan yoga.* Secaucus: Citadel Press.

Cleary, T. (1986). *Shobogenzo: Zen essays by Dogen.* Honolulu: U. of Hawaii Press.

Epstein, M. (1986). Meditative transformations of narcissism. *Journal of Transpersonal Psychology, 18*(2), 143–58.

Epstein, M. (1988). The deconstruction of the self: Ego and egolessness in Buddhist insight meditation. *Journal of Transpersonal Psychology, 20*(1), 61–69.

Federn, P. (1952). *Ego psychology and the psychoses.* New York: Basic Books.

Giovacchini, P. L. (1972). The blank self. In P. Giovacchini, *Tactics and techniques in psychoanalytic therapy.* New York: Science House.

Guenther, H. V. (1974). *Philosophy and psychology in the Abhidharma.* Berkeley: Shambhala.

Guntrip, H. (1971). *Schizoid phenomena, object relations, and the self.* New York: Basic Books.

Gyatso, T. (1984). *Kindness, clarity and insight.* Ithaca: Snow Lion.

Hanly, C. (1984). Ego ideal and ideal ego. *International Journal of Psycho-Anal., 65:* 253–61.

Hopkins, J. (1987). *Emptiness yoga.* Ithaca: Snow Lion.

Kalu Rinpoche (1986). *The Dharma.* Albany: S.U.N.Y. Press.

Kernberg, O. (1975). *Borderline conditions and pathological narcissism.* New York: Aronson.

Kernberg, O. (1982). Narcissism. In S. Gilman (Ed.), *Introducing psychoanalytic theory.* New York: Brunner/Mazel.

Klein, M. (1946). Notes on some schizoid mechanisms. In *Envy & gratitude & other works, 1946–1963.* New York: Delacorte Press.

Levy, S. T. (1984). Psychoanalytic perspectives on emptiness. *Journal of American Psychoanal. Assoc., 32:* 387–404.

Lichtenberg, J. (1975). The development of the sense of self. *Journal of American Psychoanal. Assoc., 23:* 453–84.

Namgyal, T. T. (1986). *Mahamudra: The quintessence of mind and meditation.* L. P. Lhalungpa (Transl.). Boston: Shambhala.

Singer, M. (1977a). The experience of emptiness in narcissistic and borderline states: I. Deficiency and ego defect versus dynamic-defensive models. *International Review Psycho-Anal., 4,* 459–69.

Singer, M. (1977b). The experience of emptiness in narcissistic and borderline states: II. The struggle for a sense of self and the potential for suicide. *International Review Psycho-Anal.*, 4, 471–79.

Singer, M. (1979). Some metapsychological and clinical distinctions between boderline and neurotic conditions with special consideration to the self experience. *International Journal of Psycho-Anal.*, 60: 489–99.

Stewart, H. (1985). Changes of inner space. *International Journal of Psycho-Anal.*, 66: 255–64.

Winnicott, D. W. (1974). Fear of breakdown. *International Review Psycho-Anal.*, 1: 103–7.

IV
Psychodynamics of Meditation
Pitfalls on the Spiritual Path
(1990)

The Central Way

One of the things that initially attracted me to Buddhist thought and practices was the widespread description of Buddhism as the Middle Path or the Middle Way, denoting a central course between the extremes of asceticism and indulgence arrived at by the Buddha after years of practice. Philosophically, I have also become increasingly impressed with the teachings of one of the major schools of Buddhist thought, known as the Madhyamika, or Central Way, originating in the efforts of Nagarjuna, around the second century A.D., to chart a conceptual course unafflicted by either absolutism or nihilism, two tendencies of human thought that are difficult to avoid. These two great poles, a belief in an abiding, absolute, unchanging, eternal principle (a godhead, a self or an ultimate beyond) on the one hand, and nihilistic rejection or skepticism on the other, represent the philosophical outgrowths of the human tendency to reify either the one or the zero, the Self or the no-Self, Being or Nothingness. As a way out of such limiting habits of thought, the Buddha taught that there was neither self, nor no-self (Murti, 1955, p. 7); his philosophy encouraged the de-reification (Thurman, 1984, p. 7) of both the absolute and the material. As developed by a succession of great Madhyamika scholars first in India and later in Tibet, the Central Way philosophy served essentially as a brake on the psychological tendencies of meditators at every stage of development to err on the side of either absolutism or nihilism.

In discussing the psychological risks of the meditative path, I have found the diamond-like vision of the Central Way to be highly relevant in today's climate of the adoption of Buddhism as a kind of meta-therapy by many in our psychologically sophisticated Western culture. Today, in the West, Buddhist thought and practices are increasingly looked to for solutions to many of the unresolved issues within the field of psychotherapy. While this exploration is inherently interesting and fruitful, the discussion often has centered on the question of whether meditation is therapeutic or not. This tendency, to see meditation as either therapeutic or non-therapeutic, limits our abilities to really appreciate the promise of the meditative path. The teachings of the Central Way are helpful in resolving this dilemma.

Those who see meditation as therapeutic have found it to be of use as an aid to relaxation, as an adjunct to psychotherapy, as a self-control strategy, in promoting regression in service of the ego, and in encouraging greater tolerance of emotional states, to name but a few of the most general findings. But such an adaptation attempts to fit the message of Buddhist thought into an alien cultural context, and inadvertently reveals a potential psychological pitfall on the meditative path. For, while meditation is not the same as psychotherapy, it clearly can, at times, appear to be therapeutic. At the same time, the extent to which the experiences associated with meditation can be used as a psychological defense can be significant. Any realization is vulnerable to narcissistic recruitment. It is precisely those areas that appear therapeutic that are, I would argue, potential obstacles to spiritual development for those of us who seek and set up a psychotherapeutic model for what is being sought.

On the other hand, there are those who endeavor to keep the two worlds, of psychotherapy and spiritual development, separate. They point out the potential dangers of meditation for those who have therapy work to do, the flooding from the unconscious that can be stimulated, the inappropriateness of meditation for those with problems maintaining a sense of identity. They propose a developmental schema in which ego development yields sequentially to transpersonal development, in which psychotherapy is the method of choice up to a certain point and is then replaced by meditation, which begins where therapy leaves off. This approach is best summed up in the phrase, "You have to be somebody before you can be nobody" (Engler, 1986), the assertion that the ego must first exist before it can be abandoned. I will return to this view at a later point, because it too can become a psychological pitfall, if it concretizes both the concepts of ego and egolessness. Of course, an assertion that spiritual work is only for those who have finished their psychological work, who have formed their cohesive egos, worked through their oedipal, narcissistic or infantile issues, found their identities or achieved an adequate sense of self, would likely exclude most of us. Such a position also ignores the very compelling ways in which meditation practices engage *every* aspect of the psyche, most especially those narcissistic structures that have received so much attention from contemporary psychoanalysis.

So, with apologies to the great Madhyamika scholars of the past (Murti, 1955; Thurman, 1984), I would assert that meditation is neither therapeutic nor non-therapeutic, neither an Eastern variant of psychotherapy nor something apart from the ground or territory of the psyche as we know it. What I propose to do in this chapter is to take the traditional model of the meditative path and explore psychodynamically those aspects of the psyche most affected at each stage, thereby showing what the common vulnerabilities and misunderstandings can be, and what the psychological consequences of such misunderstandings often are.

The Dual Orientation of Narcissism

The issues of absolutism and nihilism have their psychological counterparts in the psyches of most who approach the spiritual path. Both yearning for a state of narcissistic perfection and disturbing feelings of incompleteness, emptiness or unworthiness can remain prominent and influential in the minds of those who commence meditation. Such feelings may be associated with some of the most basic issues of infantile development but are nevertheless prominent even after those early stages have been successfully traversed. Margaret Mahler (1972) describes this struggle, against both fusion with an idealized other and isolation in emptiness, as reverberating "throughout the life cycle" (p. 333). Guntrip (1971) insists that "every personality" hovers "between two opposite fears, the fear of isolation in independence with loss of ego in a vacuum of experience, and the fear of bondage to, of imprisonment or absorption in the personality of whomever he rushes to for protection" (p. 291). These two poles, of grandiosity or omnipotence on the one hand, and emptiness or insufficiency on the other, represent what Lou Andreas-Salome (1962), one of Freud's great confidants, termed the "dual orientation of narcissism," that of the "desire for individuality" with its associated feelings of "a ghostlike facsimile of existence" (p. 7) versus the "contrary movement toward conjugation and fusion" that involves "identification with the totality" (pp. 4–5). Whether conceptualized as fears (of being either lost in the void or imprisoned by another), or desires (of either abandoning the struggle to maintain the self or merging with an idealized other), or beliefs (in the inherent emptiness or meaninglessness of one's being or in its self-sufficiency and inherent perfection), these two poles of emptiness and reification constitute the psychological matrix of the meditative experience, the distillation, in psychological form, of the human tendency to embrace either nihilism or absolutism.

The meditative path, through its experiences of terror and delight, of confrontation and bliss, of concentration, mindfulness and insight, seizes these psychic predispositions, engages them, and gradually works a process of understanding that obviates both extremes. Culminating in the appreciation of emptiness (*sunyata*) and egolessness (*anatta*), the meditative path is not without obstacles, generated in the most part by these two relatively intransigent and compelling notions of all or nothing.

Inner Space

Preliminary practices of meditation, just like beginning psychoanalysis, require the meditator to take his or her own experience as the object of awareness. In Buddhist terms, the attentional strategy is called "bare attention," while in psychoanalytic terms it is called "evenly suspended attention" or free association. Both require what Freud called the suspension of judgment and the giving of "impartial attention to everything there is to observe" (1909, p. 23). In Buddhist terms, bare attention is defined as "the clear and single-minded awareness of what actually happens to us and in us at the successive moments of perception" (Nyanaponika, 1962). In psychodynamic terms, this self-contemplation is defined as a therapeutic split (Engler, 1986) in the ego (Sterba, 1934), in which ego takes itself as object. As Freud commented in his *New Introductory Lectures*,

> We wish to make the ego the object of our study, our own ego. But how can that be done? The ego is the subject, par excellence: how can it become the object? There is no doubt, however, that it can. The ego can take itself as object; it can treat itself like any other object, observe itself, criticize itself, do Heaven knows what besides with itself. . . . The ego can, then, be split; . . . The parts can later on join up again. (Sterba, 1934, p. 80)

Talking of the ego like this is already asking for trouble—the word is used so often in both therapeutic and spiritual circles that its meaning has become quite diffuse (Epstein, 1988). Freud used the word "ego" in two distinct manners, without bothering to distinguish one form of usage from the other. On the one hand, he referred to the experiential "I," the phenomenological self, the part of oneself one means when one says "I" (Smith, 1988). On the other hand, he described

a "theoretical entity" (Smith, 1988), a metapsychological structure, posited to bring together a number of functions. Hartmann (1950) separated out this second theoretical entity from
the first, calling the theoretical structure "ego," and the "I"
as it is experienced the "self-representation." Other theorists,
dissecting the experience of I, have described not only self-
representations, or images of the self, but self-feelings (non-
conceptual self-experiences), and the "phenomenon of action"
(Smith, 1988) to connote the sense of agency, intention or
choice inherent in personhood. These separations have been
generally accepted in psychodynamic thought, but have not
necessarily filtered into spiritual or transpersonal discussion,
where there is some confusion as to what is actually targeted on
the path of meditation, whether it is the theoretical ego, the
sense of I, neither or both.

The primary task of the preliminary practices of meditation is essentially one of "adaptation to the flow of inner experience" (Engler, 1986). This adaptation, which can be seen as
requiring the aforementioned split in the ego, allows a kind
of inner space (Stewart, 1985; Grotstein, 1978) to be created,
a holding environment (Winnicott, 1967; Benjamin, 1988,
pp. 126–31), a "transitional space" that "contains" all of the
products of the psyche that are revealed through meditation.
Such open space is a frequent metaphor in meditation literature; its safety permits the search for authorship or agency that
culminates in advanced stages of practice.

Preliminary practices of meditation require the suspension of many conventional ego functions. No distinctions are
encouraged between inner and outer, appropriate or inappropriate, acceptable or unacceptable. Censoring of any kind
is discouraged; one is asked simply to note, without criticism
or fancy, whatever arises in the mind or body. Multiple self-

images, self-feelings, memories and self-concepts all surface, and only the synthetic ego function, or observing ego, is empowered. The danger here is of self-fragmentation, of a kind of "rupture of the self" (Benjamin, 1988, p. 61) brought on by the uncovering of defended material, the loosening of ego structure or the inability of the observing ego to "sit with" that which arises. Just as the not dissimilar psychoanalytic method has been known to encourage fragmentation, anxiety or even psychosis, so, too, can the preliminary practices of meditation prove overpowering for some. Reports of psychotic or borderline crises in beginning students of meditation indicate, in most cases, a result of this process. Those who have the most difficulty seem to lack a sufficiently strong synthetic ego function from the beginning. Meditation is not necessarily contraindicated for such people, but meditation, as it is usually taught, is not structured enough for them. In fact, they would probably do better with what beginning practices of meditation offer, the development of the observing ego, but with the method adapted for their use.

On a somewhat subtler level, the dangers of this stage of meditation for those who can withstand the psychic pressures of the opening to the internal environment is the tendency to use such practices for the purpose of doing therapy (Walsh, 1981; Brown & Engler, 1986). Refusing to progress either on the path of concentration, by focusing the mind on a single object, or on the path of mindfulness, by moving from attention to content to attention to process, the meditator can be caught up in a fascination with psychological material without moving toward any resolution of conflict. Rorschach studies of experienced meditators showed no diminution of internal conflict, but only a marked "non-defensiveness in experiencing such conflicts" (Brown & Engler, 1986, p. 189), a rather paralyzing combination in someone who refuses either to seek therapeutic help in working through the conflict or to let go of the content of the conflict as demanded by the meditative path. Alternatively, there are those who find that meditation both reveals to them their need for therapeutic work and facilitates that work by decreasing their defensiveness.

At the stage of preliminary practices, where the experience is largely psychological, emptiness may be confused with incompleteness and the image of it fused with a primitive longing. The emptiness that is most accessible here is that which Winnicott saw as originating "not in trauma, but (in) nothing happening when something might profitably have happened" (1974, p. 106). Emptiness is most palpable here as the internalized remnant of "emotional sustenance" not given (Singer, 1977, p. 461), and meditation, at this stage, provides a "transitional realm" of "open space" and "safety" (Benjamin, 1988, pp. 41–42) that allows that initial emptiness to be assuaged (Epstein, 1989).

In keeping with the psychological nature of this beginning stage of practice, egolessness, or *anatta,* is often misunderstood here as being equivalent to paralysis of ego function. Confusion over what is meant by ego can arise here, with many mistaking egolessness for abandonment of the theoretical/metapsychological/structural ego. Egolessness, in this case, is confused with the absence of repression, or with liberation from psychological defenses, a view which often encourages the release of buried sexual or aggressive longing. This can be thought of as a "primal scream" version of egolessness, perpetuated by insufficient conceptual preparation for meditation, and vulnerable to becoming a kind of self-righteous hedonism. The need for an appropriate conceptual framework at this stage is clear.

The Oceanic Feeling and the Path of Concentration

The path of concentration involves the stabilization and quiescence of the mind through the development of one-pointedness and absorption in a single object of meditation. Attention is repeatedly restricted, narrowed and focused until a kind of oneness or merger is achieved in a series of trance states known as the eight "jhanas" or realms of absorption. The experience is of progressively more sublime feelings of relaxation, tranquillity, contentment and bliss, culminating in "formless states" of infinite space, infinite consciousness, nothingness, and "neither perception nor non-perception" (Goleman, 1988). A certain degree of training in concentration, or "samadhi," is seen as indispensable in Buddhist meditation, but the development of *only* concentration is recognized as a temptation to be avoided because of the seductive and deceptive nature of these states.

The path of concentration on a single object remains the most familiar description of meditation for Western psychodynamic interpreters of the meditative experience. Analysts have tended to focus exclusively on the concentration practices, describing a process, in dynamic terms, of fusion of ego with ego-ideal, a merger with that aspect of the psyche that has continued to embody the lost perfection of the infantile state with which the person longs to reunite. This is grandiosity realized in full, absolutism par excellence. The self is cast off in favor of the "surround" (Wilber, 1984, p. 89), a progressively more ineffable other into which the meditator can dissolve. Some analysts have seen only narcissistic omnipotence shining through this oceanic feeling (Freud, 1930). Yet they understand a limitation that has always been clear to their Buddhist counterparts.

For the danger in the path of concentration is of misunderstanding emptiness as a real nothingness, of seeing egolessness as self-annihilation and of setting up an ineffable absolute as something to be united with. These are popular notions in those who begin spiritual practice and achieve some degree of meditative stability. Reinforced by the dominant psychodynamic view of meditation that has equated meditation with relaxation, this view is also strengthened by the popularity of psychedelic experiences as meditative precursors. These experiences of loss of ego boundaries and merger with a cosmic void lead naturally to an affinity with the realm of the concentration practices, but the great Buddhist teachers warn repeatedly against exclusive reliance on such an approach. Says Tsong Khapa,[1]

> We should not be satisfied with merely that Quiescence wherein the mind, thought-free, stays where purposefully focused on a single object, even where we also have clarity free of dullness and the especially beneficial joyful bliss. We must cultivate Transcendent Insight by generating the wisdom that is unmistakenly certain of the import of Thatness. (Thurman, 1984, p. 130)

The realms of the jhanas, no matter how sublime, are seen as temporary and "imaginatively constructed" (Thurman, 1984, p. 133), no different from the rest of samsara. The experience of nothingness, achievable in the seventh jhana, is clearly distinguished from that of emptiness, which can be realized only through Transcendent Insight. The danger here is in mistaking nothingness for emptiness, of remaining stuck in blissful states without penetrating their relativity.

The intimate relationship between concentration and the ego ideal becomes quite vivid when group behavior within spiritual circles is examined. For what sometimes happens is what the analysts predict: the individual members of the group replace their individual ego ideals with the same object (Chasseguet-Smirgel, 1975, p. 79) and identify with each other while focusing on a charismatic leader. This is not just a theoretical reconstruction. Individuals within spiritual groups actually *are* focusing their minds on the same objects, often symbolized in human form by the guru, teacher or incarnation that is the object of devotion. It is inevitable that such a teacher will become a repository for the projections of lost perfection from each of the devotees. United as they are by the one-pointedness of their practice, such groups are vulnerable to a collective regression in which the "primitive narcissistic gratification of greatness and power" (Kernberg, 1984, p. 15) becomes intoxicating. The psychic pressures can be overwhelming, on both students and teachers, and the activation of sexual longings as a means of literally consummating the irresistible urge to merge is virtually inevitable. The casualties of such a process among otherwise respected teachers have been reported publicly.

Surrender and the Path of Mindfulness

The path of mindfulness involves moment-to-moment attention to changing objects of perception. Rather than fixing the mind on a single object, as in the concentration practices, the emphasis here is on precise and complete attention to whatever is happening in the present moment within the field of experience. The experience is of thoughts, feelings, sensations, images, perceptions and even consciousness, arising and passing away in the endless flux that characterizes the mind/body process. Requiring a fair amount of concentration, to allow the mind to remain in the present moment, the mindfulness practices, nevertheless, do not lead to the states of trance or absorption that complete the path of samadhi. The task here is rather "dispelling the illusion of compactness" (Engler, 1986), breaking down the conventional notions of a solid, intact self, dissecting that which we have heretofore taken for granted.

The teaching vehicle of the path of mindfulness is the traditional Buddhist psychology of mind, the Abhidhamma, an elaborate categorization of all of the psychophysiological elements that pattern together to form the fabric of our psychic realities. At the heart of this system lies the notion of the five "skandhas," or aggregates, which, when incorrectly apprehended, create the illusion of an enduring self. Taken together, the five aggregates of matter, sensations, perceptions, mental formations and consciousness constitute the ground out of which we construct a sense of ourselves as something fixed, solid, knowable and real. This certainty is illusion, says Buddhist psychology; egolessness is instead a realization of the "nonabsoluteness" (Cleary, 1986) of things.

Training in mindfulness is traditionally accomplished through what are called the Four Foundations of Mindfulness: attention to the body (or material aggregate), feelings, mental formations and states of mind. Special emphasis is given to what are called the "afflictive" or "unwholesome" mental factors, of greed, anger, envy, conceit and so forth, in an effort to expose the ways in which such thoughts and emotions form the bases for our identifications.

As mindfulness develops, the experience of meditation becomes an increasingly effortless surrender to the flow of experience. Things may be changing very fast, but mindfulness, which, in dynamic terms has assumed the synthetic function of the ego (Epstein, 1988), is able to center upon the moment-to-moment process. As this ability becomes firmly established, the usual separation of subject and object tends to come undone; the "watcher" dissolves into the dynamic flow. This experience is best described as loss of "self-consciousness without loss of awareness" (Benjamin, 1988, p. 29), as ego boundaries become more permeable in contradistinction to the complete loss of ego boundaries that prevails in the merger of the concentration practices. In symbolic terms, developed mindfulness is best compared to states of erotic union in which experiences of "distinctness and union are reconciled" (Benjamin, 1988, p. 29) through the combination of heightened awareness and loss of self-consciousness.

Indeed, the culmination of the path of mindfulness is a charged state in which heightened awareness, sublime happiness, effortless energy, the vision of a brilliant light or luminous form, rapturous and devotional feelings, and profound tranquillity and peace of mind all arise together (Goleman & Epstein, 1983). An obvious tendency would be to mistake this state for some kind of ultimate, to misinterpret the loss of self-consciousness as true egolessness. In fact, this stage of meditative development is traditionally called "pseudo-nirvana" precisely because of this pitfall. As satisfying as these experiences are, they have little to do with a correct analytical appreciation of emptiness—they represent one of the more subtle variations on a kind of "grandiosity" to be found in the human realm.

The path of mindfulness is a difficult one, with potential pitfalls that can require careful guidance to avoid. At the beginning of such practice, the tendency is often to strain too tightly in an obsessive way to achieve moment-to-moment awareness. The Tibetans recognize a specific mental disorder, called "sokrlung" (a disorder of the "life-bearing wind that supports the mind") that can arise as a consequence (Epstein & Rapgay, 1989). Consisting of a paradoxical increase in anxiety and agitation, it can also have somatic symptoms of muscular tension and pain that can arise as a direct consequence of meditation. The obsessive nature of mindfulness practice can have further effects as well. The emphasis on breaking up apparent objects into their component parts, labeling them and disidentifying from them has obvious appeal for the obsessive character, who is also prone to fascination with the "interminable lists and classifications" (Murti, 1955, p. 67) of the Abhidhamma. Reinforcing character traits of rigidity, intellectualization and fastidiousness, such systems of classification historically have contributed to the ossification of Buddhist teachings and, in Buddhist India, ultimately yielded to the teachings of the Central Way. The danger for the obsessive character is an over-valuation of the discrete elements of the Abhidhamma, a substitution of the reality of the mental factors, of the skandhas, for the self that has been dissected. The correct relationship of the self to the aggregates is often confused at this stage, with the need to define or explain the self remaining paramount. Yet, as Tsong Khapa is said to have realized at the moment of his enlightenment, "it is an imperative consequence that the self is not the same as the aggregates, and the self is not different from the aggregates." The "authentic view," he found, "was precisely the opposite from what he had expected" (Thurman, 1984, p. 85).

On the path of mindfulness, emptiness is often misunderstood as a quiet or empty mind, a realm free of thoughts or mental defilements, the state of peace that comes when the discursive mind is tamed. Thoughts are in some way judged as unwholesome, the intellect is seen as the equivalent of the ego and renounced, and emptiness is confused with the vast open space that appears in the mind when thoughts diminish. There is often a search for a "'pure experience' free of concepts" without the understanding that the "conceptual aggregate is always operative" (Thurman, 1984, p. 7). In this misunderstanding, "One just refutes all views, dismisses the meaningfulness of language, and presumes that as long as one remains devoid of any conviction, holding no views, knowing nothing, and achieving the forgetting of all learning, then one is solidly in the central way, in the 'silence of the sages'" (Thurman, 1984, p. 68). But this is, again, isolation in psychological emptiness, not a real appreciation of sunyata. It is predicated on the rejection of intellect while at the same time it remains, at base, a fixed view. The point of meditation is not to dissociate oneself from an intrinsic aspect of mental functioning and substitute yet another concept. Yet this is precisely the trap that often ensnares meditators with a fair amount of experience. By holding to the view of emptiness as a thing in itself created by an absence of intellectual functioning, the meditator is, in fact, reinforcing the substratum of narcissistic emptiness that often drew him or her to meditation in the first place. This is an emptiness derived from the comparison of "this" with "that"; it prompts an attitude of renunciation, of disavowal and of repudiation in which the predominant self-feeling is insufficiency or unworthiness.

In the path of mindfulness, egolessness is often confused with self-abnegation, in which it is imagined that something real, the ego or the self, is given up. Consistent with the metaphor of erotic union, the predominant view at this stage is that egolessness results from an act of surrender, a relinquishment of the hard-won ego. This is somewhat different from the view on the path of concentration, in which the ego is seen as abolished, annihilated or extinguished. Under the spell of mindfulness practice, the operative dynamic is disavowal; the meditator feels pressure to "give it up" or "let it go." Indeed, these phrases become second nature to those on the spiritual path—the error is not in learning how to surrender or how to let go but in the reification of the "it," as in "let *it* go" or "give *it* up." The tendency to set up aspects of the self as the enemy and then distance oneself from them, be it intellect, ego, aggression or desire, is very strong at this stage of spiritual practice. Yet this is not the correct view of egolessness. Egolessness is the discovery of the non-absoluteness of that which once seemed completely real. This becomes the crucial task for the path of insight.

Clinically, many of the meditators whom I have seen in psychotherapy suffer from this tendency to dissociate themselves from that which is seen as unwholesome in themselves, be it aggression, sexual longings or rationality. Because they are seen as impediments in the realm of the ego, and because the way to egolessness is felt to be via surrender, such qualities are often repudiated, rather than noted, as fast as they arise, resulting in the rejection of vital ego functions. At the same time, the equation of egolessness with self-abnegation and the view of emptiness as a kind of beyond creates a powerful yearning in such people to be "released into abandon by a powerful other" (Benjamin, 1988, p. 131). Dissociating themselves from their own capacity for *activity*, while maintaining the view of egolessness as a state to be released *into*, creates an unending reliance on the power of another to bestow the needed state of grace. The result is often submission, either in interpersonal relationships or in large spiritual groups. Because the aggression, or desire, is, in fact, still present but is being dealt with defensively, such people often find themselves irresistibly attracted to powerful others who come to contain essential ego functions that are otherwise disavowed. Couched in a defensive gentleness and indecisiveness, such people often present themselves as ephemeral or transparent, while at the same time they depend on those who encompass just what they have forsworn to complete their worlds. The "spiritual" person who submits to an abusive spouse or a charismatic leader exemplifies this dynamic. Clearly, this is a perversion of the basic teaching of mindfulness, which *is* about the capacity to surrender to the moment, but is not, in its pure form, about surrendering unwanted qualities or about throwing anything away.

Emptiness/Relativity and the Path of Insight

When mindfulness is pursued without distortion, it matures inexorably, through the careful investigation of each object of perception, into the path of insight. While matter, feelings, mental formations, mental states and even consciousness become objects of the path of mindfulness, the *skandha* of perceptions is penetrated only by transcendent insight (*prajna*). "Insofar as apparent objects are perceived, they are the basis for sickness," said Vimalakirti (Thurman, 1976, p. 46). "In perceiving objects, we unconsciously assent to their apparent, self-sufficient, ultimate existence and thereby are confirmed in our innate phenomenal egoism," comments Robert Thurman (1976, p. 124). The *skandha* of perception involves the way in which we define our experience cognitively, identifying or naming objects and thereby no longer experiencing them just as they are. This conceptual overlay or superimposition of construct is inevitable. What is not inevitable, but is nevertheless the rule in the ignorant mind, is the mistaking of the construct for the truth. Understanding the relativity of perceptions is the essence of the realization of "signlessness" (Thurman, 1976, p. 164), in which the sign is no longer mistaken for that which is signified.

Preliminary experiences on the path of insight are often ones of dissolution and terror that serve to illuminate the insubstantiality and representational nature of experience (Epstein, 1986). The meditator actually experiences each formation breaking up. As a consequence, "the unconscious assumption of 'reality,' 'massiveness,' 'absoluteness,' 'facticity,' 'objectivity,' and so on, that we habitually impose on our perceptions" (Thurman, 1984, p. 94) is dealt a heavy blow. The meditator is said to then "perceive by way of non-perception" (p. 168), to immediately and simultaneously understand the representational nature of that which is being experienced.

The implications of such understanding for the experience of self is direct, and is best understood by reference to the work of Jacques Lacan. Lacan concerned himself primarily with the manner in which the developing infant "assumes an image" (1966, p. 2) of himself from the mirror, allowing that image to symbolize the "mental permanence of the I." This objectification of the I becomes established as an ideal that is unconsciously adhered to and which inevitably is compared with actual experience. The conception of "I" is therefore rooted in an illusory image that is unconsciously mistaken for something real. "This form," says Lacan, "situates the agency of the ego . . . in a fictional direction" (p. 2), causing the "assumption of the armour of an alienating identity" (p. 4) and creating the "illusion of autonomy" (p. 6).

When the self is investigated on the path of insight, it is this image of self, what the psychoanalysts call the "self-representation as agent," that is uncovered *as an image.* Its representational nature is comprehended in a manner that allows the continued use of such constructs, but with full understanding of their relative nature. As the Tibetan descriptions of the "aftermath dreamlike wisdom" make clear,

> there is no reification or romanticization of any state of dissolution, there is no artificial goal set for the philosopher-yogi, such as that he must "attain ego-loss," wipe out his naughty "I," and so forth. Rather he is encouraged to accept as incontrovertible the everyday conventional sense of "I," while attaining simultaneously the rational certitude of its intrinsic nonreality. (Thurman, 1984, p. 146)

The primary danger on the path of insight is a kind of self-deception in which the experiences of dissolution and voidness are seen as indicative of a higher truth that obviates the relative nature of things. There remains a strong urge to glorify emptiness as a thing in itself, to understand egolessness as an *absence* of self-representations. Here, the need to identify *something* as existing in its own right continues to manifest, and the belief in the ego as concretely existent is, in some sense, transferred to the belief in egolessness as concretely existent. In so doing, the meditator continues to subtly disparage the everyday world while looking elsewhere for release. Whether this release is seen as an attainment or a non-attainment is of no consequence; the error is the same. In the words of Huang Po, the ninth-century Chinese Zen teacher, "Why this talk of attaining and not attaining? The matter is thus—by thinking of something you create an entity and by thinking of nothing you create another. Let such erroneous thinking perish utterly, and then nothing will remain for you to go seeking!" (Blofeld, 1958, p. 86). Egolessness is not a separate state; it is only found in relationship to a belief in concrete existence.

The difficulty for those on the path of insight is to not let habitual modes of thinking corrupt the actual experience of insight and emptiness. It is easier to see ego as something that must be either transcended, through a leap into the "Beyond," or repudiated, through a rejection of intellect or "Reason," than it is to embrace the meditative path as lying *through* ego, through illumination of the representational and relative nature of that which appears to us as inherently existent. The two great poles of reification and emptiness, of absolutism and nihilism, persist in their influence even at this most subtle level of mind.

> The Centrist philosopher himself, the student of the Central Way, continually experiences little misapprehensions of emptiness as a sort of termination of everything, repeatedly confusing it with nothingness, even though he clearly knows intellectually that it is something different from nothingness. This is because the instinctual habit of reifying intrinsic reality in persons and things is so deeply engrained in our thoughts and perceptions. We *feel* intrinsic reality is "there," in ourselves and in things, and each time analytic investigation finds it to be absent, we automatically reify that absence into a little real disappearance, as if something solid had vanished before us. (Thurman, 1984, p. 158)

It is one thing to grasp the true meaning of emptiness; it is another to maintain it in the face of the onslaught of our psyches. As the Zen master Seung Sahn wrote to one of his students after a long correspondence, "Now you understand just-like-this. Understanding just-like-this is very easy; keeping just-like-this is very difficult" (1982, p. 173). The culmination of the path of insight is a constant and direct appreciation of the representational and relative nature of *this* reality. It is not a refutation of it nor is it a substitution of something in its place. Nowhere is this more visible than in discussions of ego and egolessness. Neither rejection of ego functions nor substitution of transcendent realities is sufficient for realization of egolessness. This realization must come instead through ego functions, themselves, through the kind of transformative insight that penetrates the belief in inherent existence but does not obliterate the relative.

The path of insight, at its best, does not seek to destroy the ego or to merge it with the ineffable surround—it seeks instead to illuminate ego for what it actually is. Recognizing the utility of various ego functions, it employs them to accomplish the liberation of ego from all of the misconceptions we have heaped upon it. The true understanding of emptiness allows the person to realize experientially what the psychoanalysts have only postulated. To quote one prominent theorist,

> There can be no "the" about ego, for ego is not a unity, an irreducible agency, a fixed and homogenous entity that engages in action. Ego refers rather to certain kinds of action or action in a certain mode. . . . "The ego" . . . is inherently a reified or personified concept. (Yet) . . . all strict theoretical definitions of the ego specify that it is an abstract term we use to subsume or refer to a number of functions that resemble each other in certain respects. (Schafer, 1973, p. 261)

Table 1
Dynamics of the Meditative Path

Preliminary practices: inner space
Dynamically: Paralysis of ego functions other than observing ego
Danger is self-fragmentation
Emptiness misunderstood as incompleteness
Egolessness misunderstood as loss of psychodynamic ego

Concentration: oceanic feeling
Dynamically: Merger of ego and ego-ideal
Danger is self-annihilation
Emptiness misunderstood as a real nothingness
Egolessness misunderstood as loss of ego boundaries, abolition of
     the self

Mindfulness: surrender
Dynamically: Loss of self-consciousness without loss of awareness
Danger is self-abnegation
Emptiness misunderstood as a quiet mind free of thoughts
Egolessness misunderstood as relinquishment of the ego or
     repudiation of the self

Insight: emptiness/relativity
Dynamically: Understanding the representational nature of
     experience
Danger is self-deception
Emptiness misunderstood as a real disappearance
Egolessness misunderstood as the absence of self-representations

Buddhist insight leaves the theoretical ego alone, other than to reinforce its actual theoreticalness. But through deliberate examination of the phenomenological I, of both self-representations and self-feelings, the "agent" is found to be indeterminant. This insight is in accordance with the latest psy-

choanalytic view, in which "the ego is seen as the seat . . . of inde-
terminancy" (Smith, 1988, p. 403), the dynamic equivalent of the
relativity of Buddhist philosophy. From this perspective, the
plea to all of those on the spiritual path is this, "Let ego be ego";
do not fall victim to either reification or repudiation, to either
the emptiness or the grandiosity of the illusion of narcissism.

This same argument was made much more lyrically and
persuasively six hundred years ago by the great Tibetan teacher
Tsong Khapa, who, on the morning of his enlightenment in
1398, composed an extended "salutation" to the Buddha. What
follows is but a short excerpt.

> Your position is that, when one perceives
> Voidness as the fact of relativity,
> Voidness of reality does not preclude
> The viability of activity.
>
> Whereas when one perceives the opposite,
> Action is impossible in voidness,
> Voidness is lost during activity;
> One falls into anxiety's abyss.
>
> Thus, experience of relativity
> Is most recommended in your Teaching,
> And not that of absolute nothingness,
> Nor that of intrinsically real existence.
>
> . . . Dauntless in the assemblies of the wise,
> You clearly proclaimed in your lion's roar,
> "Let there be freedom from identity!"
> Who would ever presume to challenge this?
>   (Thurman, 1984, pp. 178–79)

Note

1. The great fourteenth-century Tibetan philosopher of the Central Way.

References

Andreas-Salome, L. (1962). The dual orientation of narcissism. *Psychoanal. Quarterly, 31,* 1–30.

Benjamin, J. (1988). *The bonds of love.* New York: Pantheon.

Blofeld, J. (1958). *The Zen teaching of Huang Po.* New York: Grove Press.

Brown, D. & Engler, J. (1986). The states of mindfulness meditation: A validation study. In K. Wilber, J. Engler & D. Brown, *Transformations of consciousness.* Boston: New Science Library.

Chasseguet-Smirgel, J. (1975). *The ego ideal.* New York: W. W. Norton.

Cleary, T. (1986). *Shobogenzo: Zen essays by Dogen.* Honolulu: U. of Hawaii Press.

Engler, J. (1986). Therapeutic aims in psychotherapy and meditation. In K. Wilber, J. Engler & D. Brown, *Transformations of consciousness.* Boston: New Science Library.

Epstein, M. (1986). Meditative transformations of narcissism. *Journal of Transpersonal Psychol., 18*(2), 143–58.

Epstein, M. (1988). The deconstruction of the self: Ego and "egolessness" in Buddhist insight meditation. *J. Transpersonal Psychol., 20*(1), 61–69.

Epstein, M. (1989). Forms of emptiness: Psychodynamic, meditative and clinical perspectives. *J. Transpersonal Psychol., 21*(1), 61–71.

Epstein, M. & Lobsang Rapgay (1989). Mind, disease and health in Tibetan medicine. In A. Sheikh & K. Sheikh, *Eastern and Western approaches to healing.* New York: J. Wiley & Sons.

Freud, S. (1909 [1955]). Analysis of a phobia in a five-year-old boy. *Standard Ed. 10.* London: Hogarth Press.

Freud, S. (1930 [1961]). *Civilization and its discontents.* Second Ed. London: Hogarth Press.

Goleman, D. (1988). *The meditative mind.* Los Angeles: J. Tarcher.

Goleman, D. & Epstein, M. (1983). Meditation and well-being: An Eastern model of psychological health. In R. Walsh & D. Shapiro, *Beyond health and normality.* New York: Van Nostrand Reinhold.

Grotstein, J. (1978). Inner space: Its dimensions and its coordinates. *Int. J. Psycho-Anal., 59,* 55–61.

Guntrip, H. (1971). *Schizoid phenomena, object relations and the self.* New York: Basic Books.

Gyatso, T. (1984). *Kindness, clarity and insight.* Ithaca: Snow Lion.

Hartmann, H. (1950). Comments on the psychoanalytic theory of the ego. *Psycho-Anal. Study of the Child, 5:* 74–96.

Kernberg, O. (1984). The couch at sea: Psychoanalytic studies of group and organizational leadership. *Int. J. Group Psychother., 34*(1), 5–23.

Lacan, J. (1966). *Ecrits, a selection.* New York: W. W. Norton.

Mahler, M. (1972). On the first three subphases of the separation-individuation process. *Int. J. Psycho-Anal., 53,* 333–38.

Murti, T. R. V. (1955). *The central philosophy of Buddhism.* London: Unwin Hyman.

Nyanaponika Thera (1962). The heart of Buddhist meditation. New York: S. Weiser.

Sahn, Seung (1982). *Only don't know.* San Francisco: Four Seasons.

Schafer, R. (1973). The idea of resistance. *Int. J. Psycho-Anal., 54,* 259–85.

Singer, M. (1977). The experience of emptiness in narcissistic and borderline states: I. Deficiency and ego defect versus dynamic-defensive models. *Int. Rev. Psycho-Anal., 4,* 459–69.

Smith, D. (1988). The ego (and its superego) reconsidered. *Int. J. Psycho-Anal., 69,* 401–7.

Sterba, R. V. (1934). The fate of the ego in analytic therapy. *Int. J. Psycho-Anal., 15,* 117–26.

Stewart, H. (1985). Changes of inner space. *Int. J. Psycho-Anal., 66,* 225–63.

Thurman, R. A. F. (1976). *The holy teaching of Vimalakirti.* University Park & London: Penn. State U. Press.

Thurman, R. A. F. (1984). *Tsong Khapa's speech of gold in the essence of true eloquence.* Princeton: Princeton U. Press.

Walsh, R. (1981). Speedy Western minds slow slowly. *ReVision, 4,* 75–77.

Wilber, K. (1984). The developmental spectrum and psychopathology: Part 1, Stages and types of pathology. *J. Transpersonal Psychol., 16*(1), 75–118.

Winnicott, D. W. (1967). The location of cultural experience. In *Playing and reality.* Harmondsworth, UK: Penguin Books, 1974.

Winnicott, D. W. (1974). Fear of breakdown. *Int. Rev. Psycho-Anal., 1,* 103–7.

PART TWO

Freud

Chapters 5 through 9, directed both to my peers in the Buddhist world and to my colleagues in the analytic one, were, like those of Part 1, written to counter what I perceived to be generally accepted misunderstandings about the relationship of Buddhism to therapy. Like the notion of having to be somebody before becoming nobody, these misunderstandings all worked to keep psychotherapy and Buddhism at arm's length. Since my own experience of the two worlds was a synthetic one, I was always more interested in opening avenues of communication than in highlighting incompatibilities. This led me to look for the "Buddhist" teachings inherent in the psychoanalytic worldview and the psychological wisdom apparent in the Buddhist approach. It also kept me focused on the ways in which Western Buddhist practitioners tended to be suspicious of Western therapeutic modalities. As I would often joke, on the East Coast I needed to explain Buddhism to audiences of therapists, while on the West Coast the task was to explain psychoanalysis or psychopharmacology to those on the spiritual path. While obviously a gross generalization, this maxim nevertheless contained a kernel of truth. As a Western Buddhist psychiatrist, I needed to be able to speak in a variety of tongues.

Chapter 5, "Attention in Analysis," explores one important aspect of Freud's work, his description of what he called "evenly suspended attention." This core psychoanalytic method of deploying self-observation is virtually identical with what the Buddha called "bare attention," the meditative technique also known as mindfulness. Many of Freud's most esteemed followers did not intuitively grasp this technique, however, and sought to subtly modify it, making it more intelligible but stripping it of its implicitly Buddhist character. Buddhist understanding, I argue, actually helps to convey Freud's original intentions, clarifying his writings and returning a powerful therapeutic modality to the clinical work of therapy.

Chapter 6, originally published in 1990 specifically for the analytic community, takes Freud's well-known description of the "oceanic feeling" as its starting place. Eloquently argued by Freud, this equation of religious experience with that of the infant at the breast has had a profound impact on the way we understand mystical experience. Written for the *International Review of Psycho-Analysis,* my attempt was to put Freud's interpretation in its place. Although Freud had come up with his own version of mindfulness practice (as described above), he was not aware of its prior existence in the Buddhist world. Focusing only on mystical practices that quiet and center the mind, Freud never had the chance to analyze Buddhist insight practices, those that inquire into the nature of the self. The publication of this piece by one of the official journals of the International Psychoanalytic Association signaled a new willingness among the analytic community to take Buddhist psychology seriously and paved the way for the writing of *Thoughts without a Thinker.* A reference to this phrase, first used by the British analyst W. R. Bion, can be found at the close of this chapter.

Chapter 7 heads in a different direction. Written for an early edition of *Tricycle: The Buddhist Review,* it challenges the negative view of many holistic practitioners toward the use of psychoactive medications, specifically antidepressants like Prozac and Zoloft. In variation on the "you have to be somebody before you can be nobody" theme, many of those interested in yoga and meditation feel guilty if they find that their spiritual practices do not take care of all of their psychological needs. If they are still anxious or depressed, they blame themselves, or their "faulty" meditations, rather than turning to other modalities for help. This chapter argues against the splitting of the emotional from the spiritual and speaks of the necessity of using whatever treatments might be effective, without labeling one more "spiritual" than the other.

Chapter 8, published just before the release of *Thoughts without a Thinker,* continues to explore the issue of emotional life and meditation. Arguing against the view, endemic in some Buddhist circles, that emotions are "defilements" and that the enlightened person is "cleansed" of them, it makes the case for a more subtle transformation, one in which emotional life is not diminished but enhanced by spiritual practice.

I close this part with Chapter 9, which summarizes Freud's surprisingly keen interest in mystical experience. Disdainful though he may have been toward conventional religion, Freud nevertheless took mysticism seriously. He pondered it throughout his career, corresponded with friends and colleagues about it, and wrote about it often. While he did not know much about the teachings of the Buddha, he actually laid the groundwork for the eventual integration of Buddhism and Western psychotherapy. Anticipating many of the Buddha's fundamental insights, Freud delighted in undermining the human tendency to place one's self at the center of the universe. Like Copernicus insisting that the sun does not revolve around the earth or Darwin claiming that man bears "the indelible stamp of his lowly origin," Freud treasured his discovery that man is not even master in his own house. The absolute self, under Freud's tutelage, began to reveal its inherent unreality.

V

Attention in Analysis
(1988)

The subject of attention in analysis has received curiously little direct attention over the years, despite clear and consistent guidelines from Freud on the technique of maintaining "evenly suspended attention." This essential aspect of analytic technique has been "one of the least discussed, certainly one of the least well conceptualized aspects of psychoanalysis" (Gray, 1973, p. 474). Yet the subject has not been completely ignored. What has occurred over the years has been a steady, subtle, and very gradual shift in emphasis from Freud's original method, such that the concept has been redefined, its meaning altered, and the very words used to represent it changed. In the process, relatively little effort has gone into preserving Freud's original intent: to provide a means whereby the analyst might achieve access to his own unconscious processes in the service of analytic understanding.

In a series of papers published between 1900 and 1923, Freud was very clear about both the method and the purpose of achieving evenly suspended attention. In a parallel to free association, when the "uncritical self-observer" takes "the trouble to suppress the critical faculty" (Freud, 1900, pp. 134–136), Freud admonished the analyst to "suspend . . . judgment and give . . . impartial attention to everything there is to observe" (Freud, 1909, p. 23). Thus, Freud proposed an optimal attentional stance or state of mind characterized by two fundamental properties: the absence of critical judgment or deliberate attempts to select, concentrate, or understand, and even, equal, and impartial attention to all that occurs within the field of awareness. This technique, said Freud,

> is a very simple one. As we shall see, it rejects the use of any special expedient (even that of taking notes). It consists simply in not directing one's notice to anything in particular, and in maintaining the same 'evenly-suspended attention' (as I have called it) in the face of all that one hears. . . . It will be seen that the rule of giving equal notice to everything is the necessary counterpart to the demand made on the patient that he should communicate everything that occurs to him without criticism or selection. If the doctor behaves otherwise, he is throwing away most of the advantage which results from the patient's obeying the 'fundamental rule of psychoanalysis.' The rule for the doctor may be expressed: 'He should withhold all conscious influences from his capacity to attend, and give himself over completely to his "unconscious memory."' Or, to put it purely in terms of technique: 'He should simply listen, and not bother about whether he is keeping anything in mind.' (Freud, 1912, pp. 111–112)

Through the application of this impartial attention, not only to the patient's productions but also to the analyst's own inner experience, Freud proposed that unconscious meanings would eventually emerge in the analyst's consciousness.

> Experience soon showed that the attitude which the analytic physician could most advantageously adopt was to surrender himself to his own unconscious mental activity, in a state of *evenly suspended attention,* to avoid so far as possible reflection and the construction of conscious expectations, not to try to fix anything that he heard particularly in his memory, and by these means to catch the drift of the patient's unconscious with his own unconscious. (Freud, 1923, p. 239)

The establishment of this impartial, nonjudgmental, evenly applied attention allowed for an attunement that Freud described as follows.

> To put it in a formula: he must turn his own unconscious like a receptive organ toward the transmitting unconscious of the patient. He must adjust himself to the patient as a telephone receiver is adjusted to the transmitting microphone. Just as the receiver converts back into sound waves the electric oscillations in the telephone line which were set up by sound waves, so the doctor's unconscious is able, from the derivatives of the unconscious which are communicated to him, to reconstruct that unconscious, which has determined the patient's free associations. (Freud, 1912, p. 115)

Revisions of Freud's Recommendations

Reactions to Freud's specific recommendations for optimal analytic attention were sparse, but those reactions that did occur contributed significantly to the deemphasis on a specific state of attention that has taken place. Ferenczi, in 1919, commented on the apparent dilemma facing the analyst attempting to surrender to evenly suspended attention.

> On the one hand, it requires of him the free play of association and phantasy, the full indulgence of *his own unconscious;* we know from Freud that only in this way is it possible to grasp intuitively the expressions of the *patient's unconscious* that are concealed in the manifest material of the manner of speech and behaviour. On the other hand, the doctor must subject the material submitted by himself and the patient to logical scrutiny, and in his dealings and communications may only let himself be guided exclusively by the result of this mental effort. In time one learns to interrupt the letting oneself go on certain signals from the preconscious, and to put the critical attitude in its place. This constant oscillation between the free play of phantasy and critical scrutiny presupposes a freedom and uninhibited motility of psychic excitation on the doctor's part, however, that can hardly be demanded in any other sphere. (Ferenczi, 1919, p. 189)

This represented the first instance in which a "critical attitude" was postulated as necessary to balance evenly suspended attention, an idea that Freud never endorsed.

Several years later, Freud reiterated his basic instructions (previously quoted), adding, "It is true that this work of interpretation was not to be brought under strict rules and left a great deal of play to the physician's tact and skill" (Freud, 1923, p. 239). In the same year, Ferenczi proposed "an exception" to the rule of evenly suspended attention, arguing for "strained attention" during the narration of dreams (Ferenczi, 1923, p. 238).

In 1926, Helene Deutsch published an inspired elucidation of Freud's original concept, in which she recounted the means whereby the analyst grasps, with "analytic intuition" (p. 136), the unconscious dynamic in the patient and "reprojects" (p. 136) the material in the form of interpretations. Of note is the fact that Deutsch appreciated the role of "conscious intellectual activity" (p. 136) and portrayed it not as opposed to evenly suspended attention but as consistent within it.

Ferenczi, in 1928, continued to build on his revision by expanding Freud's use of the term "tact" (1923) to argue for a greater "elasticity" of technique. He was the first to accentuate what has become the most significant alteration of Freud's concept: that analytic attention "oscillates" between, as he put it, "identification (analytic object-love) on the one hand and self-control or intellectual activity on the other" (Ferenczi, 1928, p. 96).

Sharpe (1930) obliquely supported this idea of attentional oscillation and commented that Freud's model was but an "ideal" toward which "only approximations are made . . . by the best analysts" (p. 18). Theodor Reik made the first of several contributions to the discussion of this subject in 1933 when he argued in favor of Freud's original precepts. Urging analysts to "discard conscious directing ideas in analytic work" (p. 330), "not to cling to conscious thinking" (p. 331), and to "have the courage not to understand what his own need for logical connections, his common sense and his conscious knowledge try to thrust upon him" (p. 332), Reik argued, as Freud had, for "opening the way to the analyst's own unconscious" (p. 332).

Four years later, in 1937, Reik published the English translation of *Surprise and the Psycho-Analyst*, in which the term in translation for "evenly suspended attention" is given as "poised," rather than "mobile," attention. His chapter on "Noticing, Attention, and Taking Note" defended Freud's position that analytic insight must emerge from the unconscious, but also argued for attentional oscillation in a manner not apparent in his earlier work. Reik's primary metaphor was that of a revolving searchlight in search of an enemy, illuminating all of the territory within its range. Reik's insistence on fluctuating shifts in attentional attitudes deemphasized the implications of Freud's original stance, that a poised, psychologically balanced state of attention could be achieved by the analyst, and that such a state was useful. Reik defended Freud's position on the one hand, but cautiously reintroduced the necessity of selective attention on the other.

> Now of course it would be nonsense to declare that analysts work only with poised attention. The statement would be false, if only because at certain points poised attention must be changed to voluntary or active, when, that is to say, the significance of a symptom or a latent relation has been recognized, and it has now to be placed and evaluated. Let us return to our comparison with the searchlight: the searchlight which scours the whole foreground equally will, of course, stop at one point if the enemy is sighted there. It must be noted that

what we have here is the replacement of one form of attention by another. On such occasions, the original, poised attention gives way to the voluntary, direct form. (Reik, 1937, p. 46)

Obviously influenced by Reik's book (he cited it twice in his first five pages) Fenichel solidified the idea of attentional oscillation in the first of his influential articles later consolidated into his *Problems of Psychoanalytic Technique* (1938).

There are doubtless some analysts who would like to substitute knowledge for experiences and who therefore do not dissolve repressions but rather play thinking games with their patients. There are perhaps at least as many analysts who commit another equally serious error. They misuse the idea of the analyst's unconscious as the instrument of his perception so that they do hardly any work at all in analysis but just "float" in it, sit and merely "experience" things in such a way as to understand fragments of the unconscious process of the patient and unselectively communicate them to him. Thus there is lacking the oscillation from intuition to understanding and knowledge which alone makes it possible to arrange in a larger context the material which has been understood with the help of the analyst's unconscious. . . . The so called "tact," which determines when and how a given matter is to be revealed to the patient, seems to me not the result of a definite biological rhythm as Reik claims, but quite determinable in a systematic way. (Fenichel, 1938, p. 5)

Fenichel's bias is revealed in his statement that evenly suspended attention involves doing "hardly any work at all." His instructions on technique are extremely detailed when it comes to systematizing the process of interpretation, but his instructions on attentional method consist primarily of warnings on indulgence and a plea for the return of "reason" to the method of analytic attention.

> A constant and important task of the analyst is to steer a course between the Scylla of talking instead of experiencing, and the Charybdis of unsystematic "free floating" that corresponds to the "acting out" of the patient and is not comprehended by a reasoning power that keeps ulterior aims in view. (Fenichel, 1938, p. 6)

In an influential paper in 1942 on "The Metapsychology of the Analyst," Fliess, citing Ferenczi, argued that analysts "constantly oscillate" between "trial identifications" with the analysand on the one hand, and "reprojection" of the material on the other. Stating that the analyst can never "allow any impairment of the keen operation of any of our intellectual functions" (p. 220), Fliess portrays evenly suspended attention as "conditioned daydreaming" (p. 219) that, instead of being of paramount importance, serves only to "supplement most efficiently our rational elaboration" (p. 220). Most striking is the secondary position accorded the technique; it now serves only to supplement.

In 1948, Reik published his well-known *Listening with the Third Ear*, in English, in which his earlier chapter, previously cited, was reprinted, virtually word for word, under the title "Free-floating Attention." The one significant change from the earlier version was the addition of an early paragraph in which "poised" attention was discarded as the most precise definition and "free-floating" attention, the term used previously by Fenichel and Fliess, was substituted. Reik pointed out that Freud's original term *gleichschwebend* has the connotation of both "equal distribution" or "psychological balance" and "revolving or circling" (p. 157). In choosing to emphasize the latter, Reik supported his metaphor of the revolving searchlight in search of the enemy but obscured Freud's implication that a poised state of mind can be established in which equal and impartial notice can be given to both internal and external objects of awareness. Reik's notion of an actively roaming mind lent support for the idea of attentional oscillation, advanced by Ferenczi, Fenichel, and Fliess, and "free-floating attention" became established as the definition of attention in analysis. This shift in nomenclature is emblematic of the conceptual shift that had taken place, from Freud's insistence on a "*state* [italics added] of evenly suspended attention" (Freud, 1923, p. 239) to a broader concept of "free-floating attention" that, after Reik's book, became virtually synonymous with attentional oscillation.

Examples of this metamorphosis abound in contemporary discussions of analytic technique. The emphasis repeatedly is on the cognitive processing of the analyst, rather than on his or her ability to maintain a disciplined state of awareness. Greenson (1967) reflects this when he states, "From the evenly suspended, free-floating position, the analyst can oscillate and make blendings from among his free associations, empathy, intuition, introspection, problem-solving thinking, theoretical knowledge, etc." (p. 100). Lichtenberg and Slap (1977) continue to emphasize the broader definition that stresses oscillation when they state, "we believe the meaning of evenly suspended attention (or flexibly hovering attentiveness) to have come to encompass two main tasks: one task is taking in, resonating with, and conceptually ordering the communications of the analysand; the second task is listening to 'ascertain what uncovered material will be constructively utilized by the patient'" (p. 298). Langs (1982, p. 461) also stresses the role of cognitive processing in his definition of "free-floating attention," and Freedman (1983), in a detailed discussion of psychoanalytic listening, stresses the "rhythmicity" that exists between "receiving" and "restructuring," in which the latter is characterized by "a narrowing of attention, a reduction of the possibilities aiming toward consolidation and synthesis, and an emphasis on objectification and symbolic representation" (p. 409). Thus, the oscillation that has come to be accepted cannot even be construed to mean oscillation between attention to the analysand's material and the analyst's mental processes—it has come to refer instead to oscillation between simple listening and cognitive processing. The change is clear: Freud did not recommend several types of attention, he proposed one kind, in which "impartial attention" is given to "everything there is to observe."

Having traced the progression that led away from investigation of the propriety of the state that Freud described, it must be pointed out that his proposals have not gone completely unnoticed and unsupported. Isaacs (1939) noted the crucial role of the analyst's attention, not only to the analysand, but also to his or her own "mental processes" (p. 149) in the uncovering of analytic understanding. She described analytic insight as a "perception" (p. 150) made possible by appropriate attention. Annie Reich demonstrated consistent regard for Freud's position, referring to a "method of listening" (1950, p. 25) that constitutes the "most essential preconditions for analytic understanding" (1966, p. 345). Bion (1970) described an optimal "state of mind" (p. 31) or "frame of mind" (p. 32) in which "mental activity, memory and desire" (p. 42) are absent, enabling the analyst to be receptive to what is not yet known. "Failure to practice this discipline," says Bion (1970), "will lead to a steady deterioration in the powers of observation whose maintenance is essential. The vigilant submission to such discipline will by degrees strengthen the analyst's mental powers just in proportion as lapses in this discipline will debilitate them" (p. 52). Kohut (1971) noted the importance of selective suspension of "the intellectual activities of the higher layers of cognition" (p. 274) and emphasized that "the emergence and use of the analyst's prelogical modes of perceiving and thinking" is to be considered not a negative, passive process but rather an active discipline (Kohut, 1977, p. 251). Schafer (1983) took note of Freud's insistence on evenly suspended attention and also mentions the importance of a "disciplined approach" (p. 23) but does not specifically combine the two as Freud's work actually suggested. Chasseguet-Smirgel (1984) reminds us that evenly suspended attention provides the pre-condition for the analyst's "maternal aptitude" allowing the "capacity for pre-verbal or sub-verbal exchanges" (p. 171). Such exchanges, she asserts, constitute what Freud described as communication between one unconscious and another.

On this last point, the importance of the analyst being able to access his or her own unconscious processes in the service of analytic understanding, there is no real disagreement in the literature. (See, for instance, Deutsch, 1926; Ferenczi, 1928, p. 189; Fenichel, 1938, p. 12; Reich, 1966; Greenson, 1967, p. 364; Kohut, 1971, p. 274; Beres and Arlow, 1974, p. 28; McLaughlin, 1975, p. 367; Freedman, 1983, p. 410; Chasseguet-Smirgel, 1984.) Yet despite the fact that the unconscious is recognized as the analyst's most important instrument, the means of consistently attending to it have been neglected. As the discussion of active versus passive listening evolved, the fact that Freud's recommendations were made specifically to enhance the input of the unconscious in order to generate insight was generally pushed to the side. The maintenance of such a state, the critics seemed to be saying, is not consistent with the kind of rational thought necessary to formulate effective interpretations.

Of the few comments in the literature on the feasibility of even maintaining a state such as Freud proposed, many indicate uncertainty over whether it is indeed possible. Ferenczi (1928) stated that "a strain of this kind scarcely occurs otherwise in life" (p. 98). Reich (1950) pointed out how difficult it can be to "listen in this effortless way" (p. 25). McLaughlin (1975) remarked on how difficult it is to maintain attention and also pointed out that the way of achieving "this state of listening is quite individually determined" (p. 366). Schwaber (1983) acknowledged how difficult it is to "elucidate the mode of listening employed" by individual analysts (p. 381).

Attention in Buddhist Meditation

Confirmation for the accessibility of Freud's position comes from a curious source, given his acknowledged unfamiliarity with the psychological literature of the Indian sub-continent (E. Freud, 1960, p. 392). Yet Freud's description of the optimal analytic state of attention is remarkably similar to that described in Buddhist meditation manuals as the natural product of the steady practice of "mindfulness" or "insight" (*vipassana*) meditation (Nyanaponika, 1962; Goleman, 1977; Narada, 1956; Nyanamoli, 1976; Goleman and Epstein, 1983).

Meditation practices can be divided into two categories

on the basis of the type of attentional strategy employed (Goleman, 1977). Concentration practices stress the ability of the mind to remain steady on a single object. Such techniques provide a subjective feeling of relaxation (Benson, 1975) and, if practiced to an extreme, can produce a state of trance or absorption. These practices, where attention is restricted to a single object such as a sound, a sensation, or a thought, are related to hypnosis, both in the method used and in the physiological state produced (Davidson and Goleman, 1977; Benson, Arns, and Hoffman, 1981). As such, they represent attentional strategies with which Freud was quite familiar from his early training and interests.

Mindfulness techniques, on the other hand, build on the concentration practices but stress the ability to remain attentive to constantly changing objects of awareness. The kind of attention required is "bare attention," defined as the "clear and single-minded awareness of what actually happens *to* us and *in* us, at the successive moments of perception" (Nyanaponika, 1962, p. 30). According to Buddhist psychology, in order to maintain this attention it is necessary to attend to all objects equally, fully, impartially, and without judgment, attachment, or aversion. Cultivation of this capacity is difficult, but the process of this cultivation is the distinctive aspect and unifying theme of most Buddhist meditation practices. Intensive meditation practice usually begins (Mahasi, 1965, 1972) with training in the concentration practices. When sufficient stability of mind is attained, new objects of awareness are gradually introduced. Awareness is expanded to include physical sensations, sounds, thoughts, images, and emotional response, but the attention remains choiceless, directed always to what is predominant in awareness. The process is analogous to that undergone by Freud as he moved from an emphasis on hypnosis, with its focusing and restriction of attention, to free association and evenly suspended attention.

What is especially relevant to the preceding discussion, aside from the mere fact that the existence of such states is substantiated, is the assertion that such a mode of attention can be applied to *all* mental phenomena, by no means excluding conscious, goal-directed, problem-solving, discursive thought. While the concentration practices may very well provoke a dreamy, trance-like, relaxed, unfocused state that could be seen as the polar opposite to the state of conscious reasoning, the insight practices are specifically designed to produce a state of awareness that can be applied evenly and consistently to the full range of mental contents. To identify Freud's description of evenly suspended attention with the passive awareness of the concentration practices is not to do justice to Freud's intent. Such an identification obviously calls for some means of analyzing the raw data and processing it toward the production of an interpretation; as long as Freud's state is understood as mere passive listening, another attentional mode must be postulated.

Yet evenly suspended attention, when correctly understood and practiced, does not preclude active, logical, discursive thought. Just as in the Buddhist insight practices, it allows such thought, it makes no effort to obstruct such thought, and it pays close attention to such thought. Yet it promotes and allows a cautious relationship to logical thought, treating such mental effort as yet another phenomenon that can provide a piece of information about the truth. It promotes the ability to observe, with detached awareness, the actual mechanics of the formulation of an interpretation. Thus, instead of identifying with the thinker of the thoughts, with the formulator of the interpretation, the analyst is trained to remain one step removed. Such a stance has obvious advantages in identifying countertransference responses (Little, 1951; Kernberg, 1965; Sandler, Dare, and Holder, 1973; Sandler, 1976; King, 1978) and in distinguishing premature or inadequate interpretations, performed for the benefit of the analyst's own ego.

Traditional Buddhist psychologies not only describe such states in detail, they outline the stages involved in the development of the ability to pay attention in this way. The stage described by Freud corresponds most closely to what is termed "access concentration" in the Buddhist literature—it is essentially an "advanced beginner's" stage, requiring disciplined practice to achieve but not beyond the scope of those who put in the effort. At this stage,

> no thought or sensation is considered an intrusion. Rather, when these drift into the mind, they are observed in a detached fashion. Unlike regular thinking or daydreaming, one is not supposed to become totally involved with the mental content, but to maintain the perspective of an observer. If the meditator becomes lost in his or her thoughts, he or she again concentrates attention on the breathing, thus regaining the detached observation point from which to follow thoughts, images and emotions. Eventually, the meditator not only becomes aware of the content of thoughts and images, but also begins to recognize patterns and habits that dictate thought formation and dissolution. (Kutz, Borysenko, and Benson, 1985, p. 3)

That repeated meditation produces not only relaxation (Wallace, Benson, and Wilson, 1971; Benson, 1975; Shapiro,

1982) but also, with certain practices, enhanced attentive abilities, has been demonstrated in a number of studies (Hirai, 1974; Davidson, Goleman, and Schwartz, 1976; Brown, Forte, and Dysart, 1984a,b). The stage model of Buddhist psychological theory has also received validation (Brown and Engler, 1980). According to Buddhist sources, at the very least, a state such as that described by Freud is well within the grasp of those willing to undertake the discipline required. The similarity of both Freud's method of free association (Fromm, 1960; Engler, 1983; Kutz et al., 1985) and his method of analytic attention (Schachtel, 1969; Green, 1973; King, 1978; Speeth, 1982; Epstein, 1984; Parsons, 1984) to Eastern methods of attentional manipulation has been noted by many. That Freud should have arrived at an optimal attentional stance evocative of that of the Buddhists is not as surprising as it might seem, given his initial interest in hypnosis, his penchant for disciplined self-observation, and his reliance on the method of free association.

A Return to Freud

The crucial error made in the mainstream analytic literature in the analysis of attention is the failure to see that Freud's evenly suspended attention can encompass intellectual activity and rational thought. As Freud's view became increasingly identified with unsystematic "experiencing," it became necessary to postulate the need for attentional oscillation in order to resurrect the rational elaboration that was perceived to be missing. This has had the effect, at the very least, of establishing *two* primary goals, one to be able to freely listen to and the other to cognitively restructure (Freedman, 1983) the analytic material.

Yet rather than calling to mind Reik's (1937) revolving search-light in search of the enemy, Freud's *gleichschwebend* better connotes a pendulum, evenly encompassing everything within the two poles of its existence. It is not the oscillation, itself, that is suggested by the term evenly suspended attention, it is the state that supersedes and contains that oscillation.

Evenly suspended attention, correctly applied, does not prevent conscious thought, it merely protects against it. When paying attention in this way, the analysand's raw material, the analyst's physical, mental, and emotional responses, and the analyst's associations, need to formulate, and actual formulations *all* are attended to with the same impartial attention. The analyst need not strive to keep "anything particular in mind" because what is relevant will continually present itself to his or her mind. The analyst knows when it is time for an interpretation, not by pressing to give the correct response, but by clear awareness of the prescient information.

Freud's instructions were given primarily in the form of how not to practice. It is true that one cannot bring about the state of evenly suspended attention without working to lessen the influence of incessant discursive thought. Yet once one has succeeded in establishing this state, rational elaboration becomes one of its many attentional objects. The construction of rational interpretations is but the endpoint of a long process by which unconscious conflicts are communicated from anal-ysand to analyst and back again (Deutsch, 1926). Freud's method, and genius, was such that one state could facilitate that process by clearing the analyst's attentional field of as many interferences as possible. Such interferences, goals, ex-pectations, countertransference biases, and premature grasp-ing after interpretations obscure the "maternal aptitude"

(Chasseguet-Smirgel, 1984) necessary for perception of the unconscious. Only with the prior experience of the deeper layers of the analyst's own psyche can interpretations have their full power.

The loss of reliance on evenly suspended attention has deprived psychoanalysis of one of its most potent tools. That this loss has come from a sense that such attention does not allow or encourage the making of interpretations is regrettable. It is not necessary to postulate a distinct attentional mode specific for the conscious intellectual activity of the analyst; such activity, when appropriate, can take place within the sphere of evenly suspended attention. This attention is not just passive, receptive, empathic listening, it is a means of attending to all phenomena equally, impartially, and dispassionately, with rapt interest and active, close scrutiny but with a slight distance, so that one allows a thought or impulse to completely exhibit itself, noting all of the reverberations created, before acting.

It is essential that this attention be deployed by the analyst toward himself or herself as well as toward his or her subject; otherwise the analyst is, in Freud's (1912) words, "throwing away most of the advantage" of the analytic method. That such attention is feasible should be evident enough from Freud's example, yet the descriptions of identical states within the Buddhist cartography may be reassuring or inspiring to some who have found Freud's concept elusive or his recommendations difficult to realize. Those who reject Freud's recommendations because they do not see how such attention allows the mental activity necessary for the formulation of interpretations misunderstand the nature of the state that Freud found so essential.

References

Benson, H. (1975), *The Relaxation Response.* New York: Morrow.

——Arns, P. A., & Hoffman, J. W. (1981), The relaxation response and hypnosis. *Internat. J. Clin. Exp. Hypn.,* 29:259–270.

Beres, D., & Arlow, J. A. (1974), Fantasy and identification in empathy. *Psychoanal. Quart.,* 43:26–50.

Bion, W. R. (1970), *Attention and Interpretation.* London: Tavistock.

Brown, D. P., & Engler, J. (1980). The stages of mindfulness meditation: A validation study. *J. Transpersonal Psychol.,* 12:143–192.

Brown, D., Forte, M., & Dysart, M. (1984a), Differences in visual sensitivity among mindfulness meditators and non-meditators. *Perceptual & Motor Skills,* 58:727–733.

——(1984b), Visual sensitivity and mindfulness meditation. *Perceptual & Motor Skills,* 58:775–784.

Chasseguet-Smirgel, J. (1984), The femininity of the analyst in professional practice. *Internat. J. Psycho-Anal.,* 65:169–178.

Davidson, R. J., & Goleman, D. J. (1977), The role of attention in meditation and hypnosis: A psychobiological perspective on transformations of consciousness. *Internat. J. Clin. Exp. Hypn.,* 25:291–308.

——& Schwartz, G. E. (1976), Attentional and affective concomitants of meditation: A cross-sectional study. *J. Abnorm. Psychol.,* 85:235–238.

Deutsch, H. (1926), Occult processes occurring during psychoanalysis. In: *Psychoanalysis and the Occult,* ed. G. Devereux. New York: International Universities Press, 1953, pp. 133–146.

Engler, J. H. (1983), Vicissitudes of the self according to psychoanalysis and Buddhism: A spectrum model of object relations development. *Psychoanal. Contemp. Thought,* 6(1):29–72.

Epstein, M. (1984), On the neglect of evenly suspended attention. *J. Transpersonal Psychol.,* 16:193–205.

Fenichel, O. (1938), *Problems of Psychoanalytic Technique.* New York: Psychoanalytic Quarterly, 1941.

Ferenczi, S. (1919), On the technique of psycho-analysis. In: *Further Contributions to the Theory and Technique of Psycho-Analysis,* ed. J. Rickman. London: Hogarth Press, 1926, pp. 177–189.

——(1923), Attention during the narration of dreams. In: *Further Contributions to the Theory and Technique of Psycho-Analysis.* London: Hogarth Press, 1926, p. 238.

——(1928), The elasticity of psycho-analytic technique. In: *Final Contributions* to the *Problems and Methods of Psycho-Analysis,* ed. M. Balint. New York: Basic Books, 1955, pp. 87–101.

Fliess, R. (1942), The metapsychology of the analyst. *Psychoanal. Quart.,* 11:211–227.

Freedman, N. (1983), On psychoanalytic listening: The construction, paralysis, and reconstruction of meaning. *Psychoanal. Contemp. Thought,* 6(3):405–434.

Freud, E. L. (1960), *Letters of Sigmund Freud.* New York: Basic Books.

Freud, S. (1900), The Interpretation of Dreams. *Standard Edition,* 4 & 5. London: Hogarth Press, 1955.

——(1909), Analysis of a phobia in a five-year-old boy. *Standard Edition,* 10. London: Hogarth Press, 1955.

——(1912), Recommendations to physicians practicing psychoanalysis. *Standard Edition,* 12. London: Hogarth Press, 1955.

——(1923), Two encyclopedia articles. *Standard Edition,* 18. London: Hogarth Press, 1955.

Fromm, E. (1960), Psychoanalysis and Zen Buddhism. In: *Zen Buddhism and Psychoanalysis,* ed. D. T. Suzuki, E. Fromm, & R. DeMartino. New York: Harper, pp. 77–95.

Goleman, D. (1977), *The Varieties of the Meditative Experience.* New York: Dutton.

——& Epstein, M. (1983). Meditation and well-being: An Eastern model of psychological health. In: *Beyond Health and Normality,* ed. R. Walsh & D. H. Shapiro. New York: Van Nostrand Reinhold, pp. 228–252.

Gray, P. (1973), Psychoanalytic technique and the ego's capacity for viewing intrapsychic activity. *J. Amer. Psychoanal. Assn.,* 21:474–494.

Green, A. (1973), On negative capability. *Internat. J. Psycho-Anal.,* 54:115–119.

Greenson, R. R. (1967), *The Technique and Practice of Psychoanalysis,* Vol. 1. New York: International Universities Press.

Hirai, T. (1974), *Psychophysiology of Zen.* Tokyo: Igaku Shoin.

Isaacs, S. (1939), Criteria for interpretation. *Internat. J. Psycho-Anal.,* 20:148–160.

Kernberg, O. (1965), Notes on counter-transference. *J. Amer. Psychoanal. Assn.,* 13:38–56.

King, P. (1978), Affective responses of the analyst to the patient's communications. *Internat. J. Psycho-Anal.,* 59:329–334.

Kohut, H. (1971), *The Analysis of the Self.* New York: International Universities Press.

——(1977), *The Restoration of the Self.* New York: International Universities Press.

Kutz, I., Borysenko, J. Z., & Benson, H. (1985), Meditation and psychotherapy: A rationale for the integration of dynamic psychotherapy, the
relaxation response, and mindfulness meditation. *Amer. J. Psychiat.*,
142:1–8.

Langs, R. (1982), *Psychotherapy: A Basic Text.* New York: Aronson.

Lichtenberg, J. D., & Slap, J. W. (1977), Comments on the general functioning of the analyst in the psychoanalytic situation. *Annual of Psychoanal.*,
5:295–314.

Little, M. (1951), Counter-transference and the patient's response to it. *Internat. J. Psycho-Anal.*, 32:32–40.

Mahasi Sayadaw (1965), *The Progress of Insight.* Kandy, Sri Lanka: Forest
Hermitage.

——(1972), *Practical Insight Meditation.* San Francisco: Unity Press.

McLaughlin, J. T. (1975), The sleepy analyst: Some observations on states of
consciousness in the analyst at work. *J. Amer. Psychoanal. Assn.*, 23:363–
382.

Narada Thera (1956), *A Manual of Abhidhamma*, Vols. 1 & 2. Colombo,
Ceylon: Vajirarama.

Nyanamoli, B. (1976), *Visuddhimagga: The Path of Purification by Buddhaghosa*, 2 vols. Boulder, CO: Shambhala.

Nyanaponika Thera (1962), *The Heart of Buddhist Meditation.* New York:
Weiser.

Parsons, M. (1984), Psychoanalysis as vocation and martial art. *Internat. Rev.
Psychoanal.*, 11:453–462.

Reich, A. (1950), On counter-transference. *Internat. J. Psycho-Anal.*, 32:25–31.

——(1966), Empathy and counter-transference. In: *Psychoanalytic Contributions.* New York: International Universities Press, 1973, pp. 344–368.

Reik, T. (1933), New ways in psycho-analytic technique. *Internat. J. Psycho-
Anal.*, 14:321–334.

——(1937), *Surprise and the Psycho-Analyst.* New York: Dutton.

——(1948), *Listening with the Third Ear.* New York: Farrar Straus.

Sandler, J. (1976), Countertransference and role-responsiveness. *Int. Rev.
Psychoanal.*, 3:43–47.

——Dare, C., & Holder, A. (1973), *The Patient and the Analyst: The Basis of
the Psychoanalytic Process.* New York: International Universities Press.

Schachtel, E. G. (1969), On attention, selective inattention and experience.
Bull. Menninger Clin. 33(2):65–91.

Schafer, R. (1983), *The Analytic Attitude.* New York: Basic Books.

Schwaber, E. (1983), Psychoanalytic listening and psychic reality. *Int. Rev.
Psychoanal.*, 10:379–392.

Shapiro, D. H. (1982). Overview: Clinical and physiological comparison of meditation with other self-control strategies. *Amer. J. Psychiat.,* 139:267–274.

Sharpe, E. F. (1930), *Collected Papers on Psycho-analysis.* London: Hogarth Press, 1950.

Speeth, K. R. (1982), On psychotherapeutic attention. *J. Transpersonal Psychol.,* 14:141–160.

Wallace, R. K., Benson, H., Wilson, A. F. (1971), A wakeful hypometabolic state. *Amer. J. Physiol.,* 221:795–799.

VI

Beyond the Oceanic Feeling

Psychoanalytic Study of
Buddhist Meditation
(1990)

Although Buddhism has consistently been identified as the most psychological of the world's religions (Schnier, 1957), psychoanalytic investigation of the meditative states that characterize the actual practice of Buddhism has been extremely limited (Shafii, 1973). Freud's personal investigations into religious experiences did not include extensive experience with those of the Orient (Jones, 1957, p. 351); to the extent that they did, they were influenced almost exclusively by his thirteen-year correspondence with the French poet and author Romain Rolland, a student of the Hindu teachers Vivekananda and Ramakrishna. This correspondence, which has been rather exhaustively reexamined in recent years (Hanly & Masson, 1976; Masson & Masson, 1978; Masson, 1980; Werman, 1977, 1986; Harrison,

1966, 1979), indicates that Rolland was interested in having Freud examine the meditative experience from a psychoanalytic perspective and that Freud was excited, but perhaps somewhat ambivalent, about such an undertaking (Harrison, 1979). "I shall now try with your guidance," Freud wrote in 1930, "to penetrate into the Indian jungle from which until now an uncertain blending of Hellenic love of proportion, Jewish sobriety, and philistine timidity have kept me away. I really ought to have tackled it earlier, for the plants of this soil shouldn't be alien to me; I have dug to certain depths for their roots. But it isn't easy to pass beyond the limits of one's nature" (E. Freud, 1960).

Union

Rolland's descriptions of Hindu meditation inspired Freud to offer his well-known analysis of the "oceanic feeling" as a "limitless" and "unbounded" ego-feeling of "oneness with the universe" that seeks the "restoration of limitless narcissism" and the "resurrection of infantile helplessness" (Freud, 1930). This was Freud's only attempt at explaining meditation practice, Hindu or Buddhist, and, while it does capture some truth about techniques that involve fusion with meditation objects, it takes no account of the investigative or analytical practices most distinctive of Buddhism. What is remarkable, however, is that throughout the history of psychoanalysis, both prior to and subsequent to Freud's formulation, meditation has always been viewed in much the same manner as Freud described. The equation of meditation with preverbal, symbiotic union or regressive oneness with the mother (Fingarette, 1958; Shafii, 1973; Horton, 1974; Ross, 1975) has gone virtually unchallenged within the psychoanalytic community. The most recent qualifications of this model have focused only on whether these experiences can be interpreted as adult adaptive ones, rather than purely regressive or defensive flights from reality (Horton, 1973, 1974, 1984; Meissner, 1984; Werman, 1986). This limited view stems not from an unwillingness to apply psychoanalytic investigation to the range of meditative states but from a basic unfamiliarity with what Buddhist meditation, at least, is actually about.

Buddhist meditation actually involves two distinct attentional strategies (Goleman, 1977), the first being concentration on a single object and the second, moment-to-moment awareness of changing objects of perception. The concentration practices stress the ability of the mind to remain steady on a single object, such as the breath or a sound, for extended periods. These practices, which involve restriction of attention, are preliminary, but may be developed to the point of trance or absorption. They are always associated with relaxation and pleasurable feeling states, are the basis for the hypometabolic psychophysiological state termed the "relaxation response" (Benson, 1975), and lead directly to what Freud described as the oceanic feeling. They are also related to hypnotic induction (Davidson & Goleman, 1977; Benson et al., 1981), and, as such, represent an attentional strategy with which Freud was actually quite familiar.

The *distinctive* attentional strategy of Buddhism, however, is that of mindfulness, of moment-to-moment attention to thoughts, feelings, images, or sensations as they arise and pass away within the field of awareness. Defined as "the clear and single-minded awareness of what actually happens *to* us and *in* us, at the successive moments of perception" (Nyanaponika, 1962), mindfulness encourages insight into the endlessly fluctuating nature of the mind-body process. The concentration practices are used to provide enough stability of mind to allow this kind of exploration—but it is mindfulness that is unique to Buddhist meditation and it is mindfulness that precipitates psychological insights into the nature of the self that have not yet been explored from a psychodynamic perspective.

For, with only a handful of important exceptions, Buddhist sources were never distinguished from other mystical approaches by psychoanalysts attempting to understand such states. Focusing on the concentration practices only, analysts from Ferenczi, Jones, Alexander and Freud to Lewin, Grunberger and Chasseguet-Smirgel have repeatedly linked mystical states with prenatal or immediately postnatal harmony, union, merging or symbiosis. Freud's description of the oceanic feeling is probably the most well-known of these formulations, but the insistence on such a direct clinical correlation was as strong before Freud's declaration as it has been ever since.

The theoretical groundwork for such comparisons was laid by Ferenczi (1913) in his "Stages in the development of the sense of reality," in which he outlined the various grandiose, omnipotent and merged subject-object feelings of the infant. In a paper entitled "The God complex," Jones (1913) equated "colossal narcissism" (p. 247) with what he termed an "unconscious fantasy" of complete identification with God. Jones (1923) was also the first to identify mystical ecstasy with the merger of ego and ego-ideal, describing a "regression to the most primitive and uncritical form of narcissism" (p. 283) in a variety of Christian, Hindu and Buddhist mystical ecstasies. Schroeder (1922) clearly equated aspects of "prenatal union" (p. 447) with descriptions of both Eastern and Western mystical experiences, ascribing feelings of oneness, infinity, noth-

ingness, omnipotence and merging with the universe to predispositions of the prenatal psyche.

Alexander (1931), in a paper read in 1922 at the last Psy-
choanalytical Congress that Freud was to attend, read an analysis of a newly translated Buddhist description of advanced
meditative states. But he chose a passage that emphasized concentration, and only concentration, practices. " 'In this condition the monk is like a pool . . . ,' " he quoted, " 'filling and
saturating himself completely from all sides with the joy and
pleasurable feelings born out of the depths of absorption; so
that not the smallest particle remains unsaturated.' . . . No
analyst can more fittingly describe the condition of narcissism
than is done in this text. . . . It is the description of a condition
which we have only theoretically reconstructed and named
'narcissism' " (pp. 133–134). Yet Alexander was also the first to
recognize several essential parallels between Buddhist psychology and psychoanalysis that also intrigued Karen Horney and
Erich Fromm (1960) a generation later. Alexander referred to
the texts he studied as "psychological documents rather than
. . . products of metaphysical speculation" (p. 134), and he
called meditation a "psychotechnique" (p. 138) that enabled
voluntary access to regressive states. He was clearly impressed
with the sophistication of the texts that he uncovered, recognizing the essential psychological nature of their content.

> I will not again point out the striking similarity
> between the analytical method and the doctrine of
> Buddha. The overcoming of affective resistance
> and of narcissism, so that one is able to recollect
> instead of repeat . . . this is the doctrine common to
> Freud and Buddha. Can we regard as accidental
> this remarkable repetition in the history of both

spiritual creations whose founders both at first attempted to use hypnosis, which they found at hand
as prescientific practice? And was it also accidental
that both then arrived at the conclusion that the
chief and really difficult task is to establish the connection with consciousness? (p. 144)

The only analyst to acknowledge the importance of the
mindfulness practices per se was a man named Joseph Thompson who, in 1924, published an article entitled "Psychology in
primitive Buddhism" under the pseudonym "Joe Tom Sun" of
Guam. He not only pointed out the similarities between meditation and free association but also noted the presence of transference phenomena in Buddhist theory and began to describe
Buddhist notions of the structure of the self as seen in advanced
stages of mindfulness and insight practice. There was no further development of this investigation, however. Ongoing interest in meditation focused once again exclusively on the concentration practices.

Federn (1928) amplified the notion of the primary narcissism of the infantile state, describing a primary ego-feeling,
present from birth, that exists in an undifferentiated state and
is experienced as encompassing the world, which he called the
"ego-cosmic ego" (p. 307). He asserted that, in the adult state,
this primary narcissism could be experienced "only in states of
devotion and rapture, the highest degrees of which we call
ecstasy and mystical union" (p. 293).

Thus, by the time of Freud's (1930) evocation of the
oceanic feeling, the identification of mystical experience with
concentration practices and with the narcissism of infancy was
well established. Within the psychoanalytic literature, only

Thompson's article hinted at any further possibilities. Subsequent literature has basically reinforced the premises so lucidly put forth in the early decades of this century. Marie Bonaparte (1940) described mystical ecstasy as re-creating the "paradise of our childhood or of our dreams" (p. 437) while Lewin (1950) analyzed the ecstatic experiences of manic patients as well as those of Christian mystics described by William James and concluded that "the ecstatic mood repeats or relives the nonverbal or never-verbalized experiences of union at the breast" (p. 149). Lewin also mistakenly equated the Buddhist goal of nirvana with the Christian goal of heaven, betraying the same lack of familiarity with the mindfulness practices that had afflicted his predecessors. In clarifying Freud's notion of the ego ideal as the embodiment of primary narcissism with which an individual seeks in adult life to merge, Chasseguet-Smirgel (1975) also pays exclusive attention to mystical practices that promote a state of union, the equivalent of what she terms the "mother-prior-to-the-loss-of-fusion" (p. 217).

These traditional interpretations of meditation as satisfying the yearning to merge with an internalized image of a lost state of perfection are actually quite apt in regard to the concentration practices. Such techniques do involve limitation of attention to a single object and are always associated with feelings of delight that range from contentment or harmony to bliss, joy or rapture. In addition, they are used to provide a stabilizing force in the mind of the meditator and they are invariably associated with a sense of ontological security. The feeling state of these practices is indeed "oceanic," and the dynamic state is best expressed as a gratification of the desire to merge ego and ego ideal.

Insight

Yet the mindfulness practices are quite distinct from those of concentration, and advanced stages of such practices lead to insights and states of consciousness that have nothing to do with the tranquillity of a mind that dwells in absorption. Like free association and evenly suspended attention (Epstein, 1988a), the mindfulness practices foster a therapeutic split in the ego, encouraging the ego to take itself as object, strengthening the observing ego's capacity to attend to moment-to-moment changes (Engler, 1983). Functionally (Stolorow, 1975; Rothstein, 1981), the development of mindfulness corresponds to a development of the synthetic capacity of the ego (Epstein, 1988b), that which maintains cohesion "on more and more complex levels of differentiation and objectivation of reality" (Loewald, 1951, p. 14). This synthetic function of mindfulness recalls Janet's concept of "pre-sentification," the capacity to attend to "the formation of the mind in the present moment" that allows reality to be grasped "to the maximum" (Ellenberger, 1970, p. 376). Such a capacity allows the ego to integrate and synthesize "what seems to move further and further away from it and fall into more and more unconnected parts" (Loewald, 1951, p. 14), precisely the kinds of experiences that are detailed in traditional Buddhist psychological texts on the progress of mindfulness.

Rather than promoting the merging of ego boundaries that characterizes the concentration practices, the mindfulness practices prompt development *within* the ego itself, encouraging a thorough and relentless scrutiny of each moment of consciousness that ultimately permits the impermanent nature of all experience to be discerned with finer and finer levels of perception.

Preliminary practices of mindfulness are uncovering, much as a beginning psychoanalysis is; unconscious material presents itself and the primary task of the meditator is an "adaptation to the flow of internal experience" (Brown & Engler, 1986, p. 195) that has been shown in Rorschach studies of somewhat more experienced meditators to produce records with "increased productivity and richness of elaborative associations" (p. 180). However, as meditation progresses, there is a fundamental shift from emphasis on intrapsychic content to an exclusive focus on intrapsychic process. Thus, when thoughts occur, only the generic process of thinking is attended to rather than the specific content of thought; emphasis is on the thought's insubstantiality, its transience and the manner in which the meditator identifies with being the "thinker."

Thus Buddhist meditation is not some Eastern variant of psychoanalysis; while its methods bear some profound similarities, there is an inexorable shift away from unconscious content once sufficient attentional skills are developed. Whereas pursuit of free association leads to identification of unconscious conflict and of intrapsychic constellations such as the Oedipus, pursuit of mindfulness uncovers unconscious material but "analyzes" it only insofar as "insight" into the transitory nature of thoughts, feelings and the identifications which form the self-concept can be achieved. Because of the deliberate de-emphasis on content, insights in Buddhist meditation have little to do with drive derivatives or resistances and much more to do with illuminating the actual representational nature of the inner world.

The focus and ultimate target of this form of Buddhist meditation is exclusively the sense of "I" within the meditator. In advanced "insight" practices, attention is repeatedly brought to bear on the "sense of inherent existence" (Hopkins, 1984, p. 141), the belief in an "abiding" (Nyanaponika, 1962, p. 212) personality, or the image of an independent, substantial, permanent, "self-sufficient entity" (Gyatso, 1984, p. 163) as it is experienced subjectively. The goal is not rejection or denial of ego, nor is it an undifferentiated merger or a state of union. In contrast, through the power of the synthetic capacity of the ego, developed through the cultivation of mindfulness, the goal is explicitly illumination of what, dynamically, has been termed the "self-representation as agent" (Rothstein, 1981). The goal is not to dispel the sense of I—it remains a necessary and useful concept—but to identify the self-representation as agent as a *representation;* as an image or simulacrum devoid of *inherent* existence.

The Falsely Conceived Self

Grasping the notion of inherent existence is crucial for a correct appreciation of Buddhist meditation. It is conveyed in the psychoanalytic understanding of the self-representation as agent conceiving itself "as existing actively to pursue and insure its well-being and survival" (p. 440) and is perhaps best described as the "ideal ego," the narcissistic core of the representation as agent. This ideal ego is "the ego in so far as it believes itself to have been vouchsafed a state of perfection—it refers to a positive state even if this state, in reality, is an illusion. In fact, the ideal ego is a self-image that is distorted by idealization but it may be experienced as more real than the ego itself" (Hanly, 1984, p. 253). It is this tendency to identify with an idealized image of the self, which Lacan (1966, p. 5) has termed the "specular I" (Morris, 1988, p. 199), that constitutes the belief in inherent existence targeted by the Buddhists. The point is to experience the self as it actually is phenomenologically, representationally, rather than as a fixed entity. No longer the "shackled captive" (p. 200) of the ideal ego, the meditator, consistent with modern object relations theory (Jacobson, 1964), realizes the manner in which the self-concept has been constructed out of internalized images of self and other. "He sees the non-existence of a self of his own. He sees of his own self too that it is not the property of another's self. He sees the non-existence of another's self. . . . He sees of another that that other is not the property of his own self. . . . So this mere conglomeration of formations is seen . . . as voidness of self or property of a self" (Buddhaghosa, 1976, p. 763).

This is the essence of the Buddhist "anatta" (no-soul, no-self) doctrine, that the self as it usually appears is "falsely conceived" (Hopkins, 1987, p. 56) and lacking in inherent existence. The acknowledged goal of the investigative practices is termed "dispelling the illusion of compactness" (Buddhaghosa, 1976; Engler, 1983), revealing the self as it is conventionally experienced to be essentially insubstantial. Again, this realization is not to be confused with a loss of self or a dissolution of ego boundaries. "Selflessness is not a case of something that existed in the past becoming non-existent; rather, this sort of 'self' is something that never did exist. What is needed is to identify as non-existent something that always was nonexistent" (Gyatso, 1984, p. 40). This realization is experienced as a relief, the Buddhist texts assure us, and it forms the cornerstone of Buddhist psychological and philosophical thought.

Thus, it is the ideal ego, rather than the ego ideal, that is the inheritor of primitive narcissism most targeted by the analytical meditations of Buddhism. Responsible for subjectively experienced feelings of solidity, permanence or immortality that constitute what the Buddhists term "inherent existence," it is the ideal ego that permeates the most deeply rooted images of self. Meditation practices that produce an experience of one-pointedness, of dissolution of ego boundaries and fusion with a primary object, do gratify the desire to unite ego with that which it yearns to become. While recognizing the stabilizing impact of such experiences, traditional Buddhist psychology rejects the sole pursuance of such states. Opting instead for a very different attentional strategy, the practice of mindfulness leads ultimately to a confrontation with the most highly cherished images of the self, a confrontation that is much more likely to be terrifying (Epstein, 1986) than oceanic.

Psychodynamics

While the Buddhist practices lay great emphasis on illuminating the representational process, they make little direct effort to resolve intrapsychic conflict. Consistent with the view that the mindfulness practices reinforce the synthetic function of the ego, Rorschach studies of subjects said to be experienced in Buddhist insight practices show no diminution of internal conflict, but only a marked "non-defensiveness in experiencing such conflicts" (Brown & Engler, 1986, p. 189). Indeed, there is no method of resolving intrapsychic conflict in these practices. What seems to change in experienced meditators is "not so much the amount or nature of conflict but awareness of and reactivity to it" (p. 210). There is ample opportunity, therefore, for such practices to be used defensively (Epstein & Lieff, 1981), for libidinal or aggressive urges to be dismissed as "just thoughts" or "just feelings." For clinicians engaged in psychodynamic work with those also pursuing a meditative practice, this is one vulnerability to remain alert to. There can often be a subtle aversion in this population to such derivatives, which, it can be pointed out, is not really consistent with a non-judgmental meditative outlook but is more likely to be a defensive co-optation of the meditative perspective.

When not used defensively, the insights of Buddhist meditation can complement dynamic work by informing the ongoing experience of the self. While not challenging the usefulness of the conventional notions of I or self, these insights attack the tendency to give such notions *ultimate* reality. In bringing the representational process into direct experience, the Buddhist practices confirm aspects of object relations theory and insist that such theory can be integrated on an experiential level. Because of the insistence that the "I" that is illuminated was never intrinsically existent in the first place, the relevance of such insights is traditionally communicated through paradox or humor.

"Things are not what they seem," says a typical Zen sutra (Suzuki, 1978), "Nor are they otherwise. . . . Deeds exist, but no doer can be found." This emphasis on the lack of a particular, substantial *agent* is the most distinctive aspect of traditional Buddhist psychological thought, but such a conception is not completely outside the realm of psychoanalysis. "Thoughts exist without a thinker," insists Bion (1967, p. 165). "The idea of infinitude is prior to any idea of the finite . . . the human personality is aware of infinity, the 'oceanic feeling.' It becomes aware of limitation, presumably through physical and mental experience of itself and the sense of frustration. A number that is infinite, a sense of infinity, is replaced, say, by a sense of threeness. The sense that an infinite number of objects exists is replaced by a sense that only three objects exist, infinite space becomes finite space. The thoughts which have no thinker acquire or are acquired by a thinker."

The traditional psychoanalytic formulation of the relationship between meditation and primary narcissism is correctly conceived but incomplete and undeveloped. Buddhist meditation seeks not a return to primary narcissism but liberation from the vestiges of that narcissism. Concentration practices do indeed evoke the ego ideal and the oceanic feeling in a manner well described by generations of analytic commentators, but the mindfulness practices, which define the Buddhist approach, seek to dispel the "illusory ontology of the self" (Hanly, 1984) encapsulated within the ideal ego. In so doing, such practices encourage an intuitive understanding of "thoughts which have no thinker," an understanding which must form the cornerstone of any comprehensive psychoanalytic study of Buddhist meditation.

References

Alexander, F. (1931). Buddhist training as an artificial catatonia. *Psychoanal. Rev.*, 18: 129–145.

Benson, H. (1975). *The Relaxation Response.* New York: Morrow.

—— Arns, P. A. & Hoffman, J. W. (1981). The relaxation response and hypnosis. *Int. J. Clin. Exp. Hypn.*, 29: 259–270.

Bion, W. (1967). *Second Thoughts.* New York: Jason Aronson.

Bonaparte, M. (1940). Time and the unconscious. *Int. J. Psychoanal.*, 21: 427–463.

Brown, D. & Engler, J. (1986). The stages of mindfulness meditation: A validation study. In *Transformations of Consciousness*, ed. K. Wilber, J. Engler & D. Brown. Boston: New Science Library.

Buddhaghosa, B. (1976). *Visuddhimagga: The Path of Purification*, 2 vols., trans. B. Nyanamoli. Boulder, Colo.: Shambhala.

Chasseguet-Smirgel, J. (1975). *The Ego Ideal.* New York: W. W. Norton.

Davidson, R. J. & Goleman, D. (1977). The role of attention in meditation and hypnosis: A psychobiological perspective on transformations of consciousness. *Int. J. Clin. Exp. Hypn.*, 25: 291–308.

Ellenberger, H. F. (1970). *The Discovery of the Unconscious.* London: Allen Lane.

Engler, J. H. (1983). Vicissitudes of the self according to psychoanalysis and Buddhism: A spectrum model of object relations development. *Psychoanal. Contemp. Thought*, 6: 29–72.

Epstein, M. (1986). Meditative transformations of narcissism. *J. Transpersonal Psychol.*, 18: 143–158.

—— (1988a). Attention in analysis. *Psychoanal. Contemp. Thought*, 11: 171–189.

—— (1988b). The deconstruction of the self: Ego and "egolessness" in Buddhist insight meditation. *J. Transpersonal Psychol.*, 20: 61–69.

—— & Lieff, J. (1981). Psychiatric complications of meditation practice. *J. Transpersonal Psychol.*, 13: 137–147.

Federn, P. (1928). The ego as subject and object in narcissism. In *Ego Psychology and the Psychoses.* New York: Basic Books, 1952, pp. 283–322.

Ferenczi, S. (1913). Stages in the development of the sense of reality. In *Contributions to Psychoanalysis.* New York: Basic Books, 1950, pp. 213–239.

Fingarette, H. (1958). Ego and mystic selflessness. *Psychoanal. Rev.*, 45: 5–40.

Freud, E. L. (ed.) (1960). *Letters of Sigmund Freud.* New York: Basic Books.

Freud, S. (1930). Civilization and its discontents. *S.E.* 21.

Fromm, E. (1960). Psychoanalysis and Zen Buddhism. In *Zen Buddhism and Psychoanalysis*, ed. D. T. Suzuki, E. Fromm & R. DeMartino, New York: Harper and Brothers.

Goleman, D. (1977). *The Varieties of the Meditative Experience.* New York: E. P. Dutton.

Gyatso, T. (1984). *Kindness, Clarity and Insight.* Ithaca: Snow Lion.

Hanly, C. (1984). Ego ideal and ideal ego. *Int. J. Psychoanal.*, 65: 253–261.

—— & Masson, J. (1976). A critical examination of the new narcissism. *Int. J. Psychoanal.*, 57: 49–66.

Harrison, I. B. (1966). A reconsideration of Freud's "A disturbance of memory on the Acropolis" in relation to identity disturbance. *J. Amer. Psychoanal. Assn.*, 14: 518–529.

—— (1979). On Freud's view of the infant-mother relationship and of the oceanic feeling—some subjective influences. *J. Amer. Psychoanal. Assn.*, 27: 399–422.

Hopkins, J. (1984). *The Tantric Distinction.* London: Wisdom Publications.

—— (1987). *Emptiness Yoga: The Middle Way Consequence School.* Ithaca: Snow Lion.

Horton, P. C. (1973). The mystical experience as a suicide preventive. *Amer. J. Psychiat.,* 130: (3) 294–296.

—— (1974). The mystical experience: Substance of an illusion. *J. Amer. Psychoanal. Assn.,* 22: 364–380.

—— (1984). Language, solace, and transitional relatedness. *Psychoanal. Study Child,* 39: 167–194.

Jacobson, E. (1964). *The Self and the Object World.* New York: Int. Univ. Press.

Jones, E. (1913). The God complex. In *Essays in Applied Psychoanalysis II.* London: Hogarth Press, 1951.

—— (1923). The nature of auto-suggestion. In *Papers on Psychoanalysis.* Boston: Beacon Press, 1948.

—— (1957). *Sigmund Freud: Life and Work, Vol. III, The Last Phase, 1919–1939.* London: Hogarth Press.

Lacan, J. (1966). *Ecrits: A Selection.* New York: W. W. Norton, 1977.

Lewin, B. D. (1950). *The Psychoanalysis of Elation.* New York: W. W. Norton.

Loewald, H. W. (1951). Ego and reality. *Int. J. Psychoanal.,* 32: 10–18.

Masson, J. (1980). *The Oceanic Feeling: The Origins of Religious Sentiment in Ancient India.* Dordrecht, Holland: D. Reidel.

—— & Masson, T. C. (1978). Buried memories on the acropolis: Freud's relation to mysticism and anti-Semitism. *Int. J. Psychoanal.,* 59: 199–208.

Meissner, W. W. (1984). *Psychoanalysis and Religious Experience.* New Haven and London: Yale Univ. Press.

Morris, H. (1988). Reflections on Lacan: His origins in Descartes and Freud. *Psychoanal. Q.,* 57: 186–207.

Nyanaponika Thera (1962). *The Heart of Buddhist Meditation.* New York: S. Weiser.

Ross, N. (1975). Affect as cognition: With observations on the meaning of mystical states. *Int. Rev. Psychoanal.,* 2: 79–93.

Rothstein, A. (1981). The ego: An evolving construct. *Int. J. Psychoanal.,* 62: 435–445.

Schnier, J. (1957). The Tibetan Lamaist ritual: Chod. *Int. J. Psychoanal.,* 38: 402–407.

Schroeder, T. (1922). Prenatal psychisms and mystical pantheism. *Int. J. Psychoanal.,* 3: 445–466.

Shafii, M. (1973). Silence in service of the ego: Psychoanalytic study of meditation. *Int. J. Psychoanal.,* 54: 431–443.

Stolorow, R. D. (1975). Toward a functional definition of narcissism. *Int. J. Psychoanal.*, 56: 179–185.

Sun, Joe Tom (1924). Psychology in primitive Buddhism. *Psychoanal. Rev.*, 11: 38–47.

Suzuki, D. T. (1978). *The Lankavatara Sutra.* Boulder, Colo.: Prajna Press.

Werman, D. S. (1977). Sigmund Freud and Romain Rolland. *Int. Rev. Psychoanal.*, 4: 225–242.

—— (1986). On the nature of the oceanic experience. *J. Amer. Psychoanal. Assn.*, 34: 123–139.

VII
Awakening with Prozac
Pharmaceuticals and Practice
(1993)

D
espite ten years of dharma practice and five years of psychotherapy, Leslie was still miserable. To those who knew her casually, she did not seem depressed, but with her close friends and lovers she was impossibly demanding. Subject to brooding rages when she felt the least bit slighted, Leslie had alienated most of the people in her life who had wanted to be close to her. Unable to control her frustration when sensing a rejection, she would withdraw in anger, eat herself sick, and take to her bed. When her therapist recommended that she take the antidepressant Prozac she was insulted, feeling that such an action would violate her Buddhist precepts.

There is a story in the ancient Buddhist texts that relates how the King of Kosala once told the Buddha that unlike disciples of other religious systems who looked haggard, coarse, pale, and emaciated, his disciples appeared to be "joyful and elated, jubilant and exultant, enjoying the spiritual life, with faculties pleased, free from anxiety, serene, peaceful, and living with a gazelle's mind." The idea that the Buddha's teachings ought to be enough to bring about such a delightful mental state continues to be widespread in contemporary Buddhist circles. For many, Buddhist meditation has all of the trappings of an alternative psychotherapy, including the expectation that intensive practice should be enough to turn around any objectionable emotional experience. Yet the unspoken truth is that many experienced dharma students, like Leslie, have found that disabling feelings of depression, agitation, or anxiety persist despite a long commitment to Buddhist practice. This anguish is often compounded by a sense of guilt about such persistence and a sense of failure at not "making it" as a student of the dharma when afflicted in this way. This situation is analogous to that in which a devotee of natural healing is stricken with cancer, despite eating natural foods, exercising, meditating, and taking vitamins and herbs. As Treya Wilber pointed out in an article written before her early death from breast cancer, the idea that we should take responsibility for all of our illnesses has its limits.

"Why did you choose to give yourself cancer?" she reported many of her "New Age" friends asking her, provoking feelings of guilt and recrimination that echo much of what dharma students with depression often feel. More sensitive friends approached her with the slightly less obnoxious question "How are you choosing to use this cancer?" which, in her own words, allowed her to "feel empowered and supported and challenged in a positive way." With physical illness it is perhaps a bit easier to make this shift; with mental illness one's identification is often so great that it is extremely difficult to see mental pain as "not I," as symptomatic of treatable illness rather than evocative of the human condition.

Of course, the First Noble Truth asserts the universality of *dukkha*, suffering or, in a better translation, pervasive unsatisfactoriness. Is the hopelessness of depression, the pain of anxiety, or the discomfort of dysphoria simply a manifestation of *dukkha*, or do we do ourselves and the dharma a disservice to expect any kind of mental pain to dissolve once it becomes an object of meditative awareness? The great power of Buddhism lies in its assertion that all of the stuff of the neurotic mind can become fodder for enlightenment, that liberation of the mind is possible without resolution of all the neuroses. Many Westerners feel an immediate relief in this view. They find they are accepted by their dharma teachers as they are, and this attitude of unconditional acceptance and love is one that evokes deep appreciation and gratitude. This is a priceless contribution of Buddhist psychology—it offers the potential of transforming what often becomes a stalemate in psychotherapy, when the neurotic core is exposed but nothing can be done to eradicate it.

Eden's situation typifies this. A writer whose crisis manifested in her twenty-ninth year, Eden suffered from an oppressive feeling of emptiness or hollowness for much of her adult life. Already a veteran of ten years of intensive psychotherapy, she understood that her feelings of numbness and yearning stemmed from emotional neglect in her youth. Her father, a cold and aloof physician, had avoided the children and retreated to a rarefied intellectual world of scientific research, while her mother was fiercely loving and protective but indiscriminate in her attention, praising Eden for anything and everything and leading her to distrust her mother's affection altogether. Eden was angry and demanding in her interpersonal relationships, impatient with any perceived flaw, with any inability of her partner to satisfy all of her needs. She had recognized the source of her problem through psychotherapy but had found no relief; she continued to idealize and then devalue her lovers and could not sustain an intimate relationship.

Eden's inner emptiness was a good example of what the psychoanalyst Michael Balint (1968) has called the regret of the basic fault. "The regret or mourning I have in mind is about the unalterable fact of a defect or fault in oneself which, in fact, had cast its shadow over one's whole life, and the unfortunate effects of which can never fully be made good. Though the fault may heal, its scar will remain forever; that is, some of its effects will always be demonstrable" (p. 183). No antidepressants were effective in Eden's case. In order for her to find some relief she had to confront directly her inner feeling of emptiness with the understanding that she was yearning for something that would no longer prove satisfying. Having missed a critical kind of attention relevant only to a child, she found that if someone tried to give her that as an adult, it felt oppressive and suffocating. Only through the tranquil stabilization of meditation could she stand the anxiety of this inner feeling of emptiness without reacting violently against it.

This illustrates the Buddhist approach. A person must find the courage and mental balance to confront the neurotic core or "basic fault" through the discipline of meditative awareness. In the Buddhist view, all of the elements of personality have the potential to become vehicles for enlightenment, all the waves of the mind are but an expression of the ocean of big mind. Mental illness is not an especially developed concept in Buddhist thought, except in an existential sense, where it is exquisitely developed. Buddhist texts speak of the two sicknesses: an internal sickness consisting of a belief in a permanent and eternal self, and an external sickness consisting of a grasping for a real object. The focus, in Buddhist psychology, is always on the existential plight of the subjective ego, articulated especially well by Richard De Martino in the classic *Zen Buddhism and Psychoanalysis* (1960), co-written with Erich Fromm and D. T. Suzuki:

> Object-dependent and object-conditioned, the ego is, further, object-obstructed. In the subjectivity in which it is aware of itself, the ego is at the same time separated and cut off from itself. It can never, as ego, contact, know or have itself in full and genuine individuality. Every such attempt removes it as an ever regressing subject from its own grasp, leaving simply some object semblance of itself. Continually elusive to itself, the ego has itself merely as object. Divided and dissociated in its centeredness, it is beyond its own reach, obstructed, removed and alienated from itself. Just in having itself, it does not have itself. (p. 146)

It is this existential longing for meaning or completion and the inner feelings of emptiness, hollowness, isolation, fear, anxiety, or incompleteness that Buddhist psychology approaches most directly. Depression, as a critical entity, is rarely addressed. The fifty-two mental factors of the Abhidhamma (the psychological texts of traditional Buddhism), for example, list a compendium of afflictive emotions such as greed, hatred, conceit, envy, doubt, worry, restlessness, and avarice, but do not even include sadness except as a kind of unpleasant feeling that can tinge other mental states. Depression is not mentioned.

Mind is described in the traditional Abhidhamma as a sense organ, or "faculty," like the eye, ear, nose, tongue, or body, that perceives concepts or other mental data, surveys the fields of the other sense organs, and is subject to "obscurations," veils of afflictive emotions that obscure the mind's true nature. The faculty of mind and the consciousness produced by it are seen as the primary source of the feeling of "I am" that is then presumed to be real. There is little discussion in Buddhist literature, however, of the mind's propensity toward disruptions that cannot be remedied through spiritual practice alone. As Buddhism evolved, its emphasis became even more focused on discovering the "true nature" of mind, rather than bothering with discussions of mental illness. This "true nature" is mind revealed as naturally empty, clear, and unimpeded. The thrust of meditation practice became the experience of mind in this natural state.

"Ultimately speaking," wrote the late Tibetan meditation master Kalu Rinpoche (1986),

> the causes of samsara are produced by the mind, and mind is what experiences the consequences. Nothing other than mind makes the universe, and nothing other than mind experiences it. Yet, still ultimately speaking, mind is fundamentally empty, no "thing" in and of itself. To understand that the mind producing and experiencing samsara is nothing real in itself can actually be a source of great relief. If the mind is not fundamentally real, neither

are the situations it experiences. By finding the
empty nature of mind and letting it rest there, we
can find much relief and relaxation amidst the turmoil, confusion, and suffering that constitute the
world. (p. 29)

A glimpse of this reality can be quite transformative
from a psychotherapeutic point of view, but quite elusive for
those who do not have the capacity to let their mind rest in its
natural state because of the depths of their anxieties, depressions, or mental imbalances.

Timothy was a successful photographer whose life suddenly unraveled one year. His therapist of four years died
unexpectedly of a heart attack, his wife was diagnosed with
breast cancer and needed both surgery and chemotherapy, and
his dealer suddenly went bankrupt, closed her gallery, and
folded without paying him the thousands of dollars that he
was owed. His studio felt contaminated by anxious hours on
the telephone with his wife and her doctors; he could no
longer take refuge there and what was the point, anyway, without a dealer to sell his work? He was immersed in meaninglessness, death, and grief and he began to worry obsessively about
his own health. With no active spiritual practice, Timothy
lacked a context in which to place the suffering that had suddenly overwhelmed him, found no means of being in his pain
while still actively living, and had little ability to be there for
his wife's trauma.

Reluctantly, he went with his wife to a workshop on
coping with serious illness by Jon Kabat-Zinn, which generated
an interest in Buddhist practice. Slowly, he rediscovered his
vitality and took possession of his studio once again while
relating to his wife in a way that his unexamined grief had

prevented him from doing previously. More than anything else, his dharma practice seemed to give him a method of experiencing mental agony without succumbing to the incredible pain that it produced. His was a situation in which medication would have missed the point. His crisis was an existential or spiritual one as much as a case of unexplored grief, and he was able to find a bit of the relief that Kalu Rinpoche refers to.

The wish that meditation could, by itself, prove to be some kind of panacea for all mental suffering is widespread and certainly understandable. The psychiatrist Roger Walsh remembers an early retreat at which he had the opportunity to watch Ram Dass be with a young man who had become psychotic in the midst of his practice. "Oh, good," he remembers thinking. "Now I'll get to see Ram Dass deal with a psychotic person in a spiritual way." After watching Ram Dass chanting with the young man and trying to center him meditatively, Walsh observed that it was necessary to restrain him because of his increasing agitation and violence. At this point, the young man bit Ram Dass in the stomach, prompting an immediate call for Thorazine, a potent anti-psychotic drug. The desire to avoid medication when doing spiritual practice, to confront the mind in its naked state, is certainly a noble one, but it is not always realistic.

There continues to be a widespread suspicion of pharmacological treatments for mental anguish in dharma circles, a prejudice against using drugs to correct mental imbalance. Just as the cancer patient is urged to take responsibility for something that may be beyond her control, the depressed dharma student is all too often given the message that no pain is too great to be confronted on the zafu, that depression is the equivalent of mental weakness or lassitude, that the problem is in the quality of one's practice rather than in one's body. I remember those prejudices from my early psychiatric training. I was quite suspicious of all the psychotropic drugs, equating Lithium with the anti-psychotics like Thorazine which mask or suppress psychotic symptoms but do not correct the underlying schizophrenic condition. One of the most concrete things that I learned in those years of training was that there actually are several psychiatric conditions which can be cured or prevented through the use of medications and that denial of such treatment is folly. This is not to say that it is always so clear when a problem is chemical, when it is psychological, or when it is spiritual. There are no blood tests for depression, for example. And yet, the presence of certain constellations of symptoms invariably point to a treatable condition that is unlikely to resolve through spiritual practice alone.

Peggy came to dharma practice in her early twenties while seriously depressed. Adrift in the counterculture, estranged from her divorced, alcoholic, and abusive mother, tenuously bound to her self-involved and indulgent father, she was contemplating suicide when she came upon her first dharma teacher in San Francisco. She felt "found" by that teacher, surrendered the idea of suicide, and threw herself into dharma practice for the next seventeen years. She became gradually disillusioned by a succession of teachers, however, getting to know enough of them personally to lose any ability to idealize them in the way she had originally. When her mother became ill with cancer, a five-year relationship broke up, and her best friend had a baby as Peggy approached her fortieth birthday, she became increasingly withdrawn and agitated. She felt tired and anxious, weak and lethargic but unable to sleep, filled with hateful thoughts and obsessive ruminations, and unable to concentrate on her work or her dharma practice. She took to her bed, lost interest in her friends, and began to imagine that she was already dead. Her friends took her to a spiritual community, to a number of healers, and to several respected Buddhist teachers who finally referred her for psychiatric help. As it turned out, there was a history of depression on her mother's side of the family. Peggy was convinced she was doomed to repeat her mother's deterioration; she felt she had failed as a Buddhist and yet was resistant to seeing her depression as a condition that warranted treatment with medication. She got better after about four months of taking antidepressants, which she took for a year and has not needed since. While depressed, she was simply unable to muster the concentration necessary to meditate effectively; the "ultimate view" that Kalu Rinpoche describes was unavailable to her consciousness.

The psychiatric tradition with the most experience in differentiating existential from biological mental illness is probably the Tibetan one, which developed in a culture and society completely immersed in the theory and practice of Buddhism. The Tibetan medical authorities recognize a host of "mental illnesses," it turns out, for which they recommend pharmaceutical, not meditative, interventions, including many that correspond to Western diagnoses of depression, melancholia, panic, manic-depression, and psychosis. Not only do they not always counsel meditation as a first line of treatment, they also recognize that meditation can often make such conditions worse. Indeed, it is well known that meditation, itself, can provoke a psychiatric condition, an obsessive anxiety state, which is a direct result of trying to force the mind in a rigid and unyielding way to stay on the object of awareness. According to the late Terry Clifford in her book *Tibetan Buddhist Medicine and Psychiatry* (1984), the Tibetan tradition holds that these medical teachings were expounded by the manifestation of Buddha in the form of Vaidurya in the mystical medicine paradise called Tanatuk, literally, "Pleasing When Looked Upon." Here Vaidurya is said to have commented that "all people who want to meditate and reach nirvana and want health, long life, and happiness should learn the science of medicine." Treatments for mental illnesses are not antithetical to dharma practice; rather, the Tibetan teachings seem to say, they can be venerated as manifestations of the Medicine Buddha himself.

Yet many of today's dharma students who suffer from such mental illnesses have trouble identifying effective treatments as manifestations of the Medicine Buddha. They seem to prefer to regard their symptoms as manifestations of the Buddha-mind. A recent patient of mine, for example, was a brilliant conceptual mathematician named Gideon who taught on the graduate level and was a proud, willful, creative man who had gravitated toward Buddhist practice while in graduate school. He had suffered one "nervous breakdown" during that time: for a six-month period he had become restless and agitated with bursts of creative energy, a racing mind in which thoughts tumbled one on top of the next, a labile mood in which laughter and tears were never far from each other, and a profound difficulty in sleeping. He finally "crashed," spent a week in the hospital, and emerged with no further difficulty for the next five years. He had several depressive episodes in his thirties, during which time he became much less productive in his work, felt sad and withdrawn, and retreated in a kind of uneasy solitude. He was vehemently anti-medication, however, and weathered those depressions by closing himself into his apartment and lying in his darkened room. Again, the episodes passed, and Gideon was able to continue his work. In his forties, he had a succession of episodes, much like the nervous breakdown of his graduate years, in which he also became paranoid, hearing special messages sent to him through the television and radio warning him of a conspiracy. Psychiatric hospitalization was required after he was moved to take cover in Central Park.

Gideon's condition was manic-depression, an episodic mood disturbance that usually first manifests in young adulthood and can cause either recurrent depressions, ecstatic highs, or some combination thereof. It is characteristic of this illness that the episodes come and go, with the person returning to an unaffected state between episodes. Many people with this illness find that the episodes are fully preventable or at least markedly diminished by the daily intake of Lithium salt. Gideon was markedly resistant to the idea that he had this illness, however, and he was equally resistant to the idea of taking Lithium, quoting the dharma to the effect of "letting the mind rest in its natural state" to support his refusal to take medication. The manic episodes came rapidly in Gideon's forties, hitting him every year or so and effectively ruining his academic career. For a while, his family attempted to put medication in his food without his knowledge, an endeavor which only supported his paranoia, but to this day he has refused to take medication voluntarily. He remains a brilliant and proud man with the ability to work productively between episodes, but the illness has been destabilizing him relentlessly.

Through these examples I mean to make the point that neither meditation nor medication is uniformly beneficial in every case of mental suffering. Meditation practice can be enormously helpful or can contribute to the force of denial. There is a continuing ignorance in dharma circles of the benefits to be had from psychiatric treatments, just as there is a corresponding ignorance in traditional psychiatric circles of the benefits to be had from meditation practice.

In addition, there is an uncomfortable parallel in the history of psychoanalysis to the current prejudice against pharmacological treatments in dharma circles. Freud's initial group of followers and adherents were the intellectual radicals of their day. Their excitement and faith in this new and profound method of treatment led them to embrace it as a panacea in much the same way that our contemporary avant-garde has embraced Buddhist practice. The daughter of Louis Comfort Tiffany, Dorothy Burlingham, a seminal New York figure of the early 1900s, for example, left her manic-depressive husband after his relentless and unending series of breakdowns and took her four young children to Vienna in 1925 to seek analysis with Freud. Eventually moving into the apartment below Freud's, Dorothy Burlingham began a lifelong relationship with the Freud family that evolved into her living with Anna Freud for the rest of her life (she died in 1979). Anna Freud became her children's analyst, but at least one of them, her son Bob, seems to have inherited the manic-depressive illness from his father. In a tragic story outlined by Ms. Burlingham's grandson Michael John Burlingham in his book *The Last Tiffany* (1989), Bob suffered from unmistakable manic and depressive episodes and died an early death at the age of fifty-four. So great was Anna Freud's belief in psychoanalysis, however, that even when Lithium was discovered as an effective prophylactic treatment, she would not consider its use. He was only permitted treatment that lay within the parameters of Freudian ideology, an approach notoriously ineffective for his condition.

There are undoubtedly dharma practitioners who are depriving themselves in the same way, out of a similar faith in the universality of their ideology. Such people would do well to remember the Buddha's teachings of the Middle Path, especially his counsel against the search for happiness through self-mortification in different forms of asceticism, which he called "painful, unworthy, and unprofitable." To suffer from psychiatric illness willfully, when treatment is mercifully available, is but a contemporary ascetic practice. The Buddha himself tried such ascetic practices, but gave them up. His counsel is worth keeping.

References

Balint, M. (1968). *The Basic Fault: Therapeutic Aspects of Regression.* London: Tavistock.

Burlingham, M. (1989). *The Last Tiffany: A Biography of Dorothy Burlingham.* New York: Atheneum.

Clifford, T. (1984). *Tibetan Buddhist Medicine and Psychiatry.* York Beach, Maine: Samuel Weiser.

DeMartino, R. (1960). The human situation and Zen Buddhism. In E. Fromm, D. T. Suzuki and R. DeMartino (eds.), *Zen Buddhism and Psychoanalysis.* New York: Harper and Row.

Rinpoche, K. (1986). *The Dharma That Illuminates All Beings Impartially Like the Light of the Sun and the Moon.* Albany: State University of New York Press.

VIII
A Buddhist View of Emotional Life
(1995)

I remember once, not so many years ago, sitting in my therapist's office, telling him of an argument that I had had with someone close to me. I can no longer bring back the details, but I had done something to get my friend upset with me, and she had become quite angry—unjustifiably and disproportionately in my view. I remember feeling upset and frustrated as I recounted the events.

"All I can do is love her more strongly at those times," I insisted somewhat plaintively, drawing on my years of meditation practice and the sincerity of my deeper feelings.

"That will never work," he snapped, and it was like being hit with a Zen master's stick. He looked at me somewhat quizzically, as if amazed at my foolishness. "What's wrong with being angry?" he said.

This interaction has stayed with me for years because, in some way, it crystallizes the difficulties that we face in trying to integrate Buddhist and Western psychological approaches. Buddhism gives us a mixed message about the emotions, on the one hand supporting the notion that we must strive to eliminate them, and on the other hand teaching acceptance of whatever arises. *Is* there something wrong with being angry? *Can* we get rid of it? What does it mean to *work it through?* I have to address questions like this over and over again in my work as a therapist, where it has become clear to me that *working through* an emotion like anger often means something different from merely eliminating it. For, as the Buddhist view has consistently demonstrated, it is the perspective of the sufferer that determines whether a given experience perpetuates suffering or is a vehicle for awakening. To work something through means to change one's view; if we try instead to change the emotion, we may achieve some short-term success, but we remain bound by forces of attachment and aversion to the very feelings from which we are struggling to be free.

Of course, my desire to replace my difficult feelings with their opposite was not an original idea. It derived in my case from the Buddhist psychology of the *abhidhamma*, the earliest psychological writings of Buddhism. There exists in most of us the desire to be free from the pressures of our emotions, to cast off the constraints of our emotional lives and replace the problematic feelings with their less conflicted opposites. There is a universal tendency toward debasement in the sphere of the emotions, it seems. We assume that the only way to be free of suffering is to be completely rid of it.

This longing for a realm of emotional quiescence has had an important impact on the way we practice Buddhism. The very teachings themselves often seem to suggest that this is the model that we must strive to achieve. Certain emotions are unwholesome, the *abhidhamma* teaches. We must do whatever we can to diminish their influence in our minds. Consequently, when we read the stories of Buddhist teachers freely expressing sadness or rage, we become confused. These stories contradict the more formal teachings of Buddhism and force us to reevaluate our unconscious assumptions about how loathsome the emotions must be. Our willingness to believe in a model that denies a place for the emotions derives in part from the unconscious desire to split off the emotions from the rest of our experience, to make them the culprits for our predicament. If we could but root out and destroy our emotional natures, we think, we could be following in the footsteps of the Buddha.

This desire to destroy the offending emotions is also one that is very common in people seeking psychotherapy. Just as many meditators assume that proper meditation means diminution of feeling, so many people entering psychotherapy demonize the unwanted emotions that propel them to seek help. After breaking up his ten-year marriage, for instance, a good friend of mine sought psychotherapy at a local mental health clinic. His only wish, he told his new therapist, was to be free from what he was feeling. He implored his therapist to take his pain away, to rid him of his unwanted emotions.

His therapist, however, had just left a Zen community where she had been in residence for three years. When my friend approached her with his pain, she urged him only to stay with his feelings, no matter how unpleasant they were. She did not attempt to reassure him or to help him change what he was feeling. When he would complain of his anxiety or his loneliness, she would encourage him to feel them more intensely. While my friend did not feel any better, he was intrigued by his therapist's approach and began to practice meditation. He describes one pivotal moment in his meditation as the point in which his depression began to clear.

Terribly uncomfortable with the itchings, burnings, and

pains of his practice, and unable to simply stay with the sensations, he remembers finally watching an itch develop, crest, and disappear without scratching it. In so doing, he says, he suddenly realized what his therapist had meant when she counseled him to stay with his emotional state, and from that moment on his depression began to lift. His feelings began to change only when he stopped wishing them to.

There are schools of thought—within both Buddhism and psychoanalysis—that do not readily admit to the possiblity of an emotional transformation such as my friend experienced. Both orthodox psychoanalysts and fundamentalist Buddhists see the emotions as coercive forces which are, by their very nature, threatening, destabilizing, and potentially overwhelming. The best one can do with these passions, according to this view, is to control, master, or—in the Buddhist view at least—extinguish them. The common thread is that the passions are viewed as dark forces with wills of their own that must be strictly regulated. A successful graduate of a psychoanalysis influenced by this view is someone who has uncovered all of her primitive emotion, but has learned how to keep it from interfering with mature satisfactions. A successful practitioner of a Buddhism influenced by this view is imagined to be someone whose emotions no longer disturb a pervasive equanimity. This is why we can be so puzzled to read of the Tibetan yogi Marpa weeping at the death of his son. Why has he not transcended his emotion?

There exists within both Buddhism and psychoanalysis another perspective on the emotions, however, one that senses the possibility of transformation rather than transcendence. In this view, the passions are not necessarily set up as the enemy; they are treated more like a long-lost cousin. By allowing them access to consciousness, the emotions cease to be felt as an alien force, but come to be experienced as an inseparable part of a larger whole. In so doing, the emotions are permitted to spontaneously mature, a process that my friend caught a glimpse of through his meditation.

Freud described this process as sublimation (1910a). Sublimation, for Freud, held out the possibility of escape from the impossible demands of the "infantile wishful impulses," but did not mean that the passions, themselves, were inherently dangerous. Listen, for instance, to Freud's description of Leonardo da Vinci:

> His affects were controlled. . . ; he did not love and hate, but asked himself about the origin and significance of what he was to love or hate. Thus he was bound at first to appear indifferent to good and evil, beauty and ugliness. . . . In reality Leonardo was not devoid of passion. . . . He had merely converted his passion into a thirst for knowledge. . . . When, at the climax of a discovery, he could survey a large portion of the whole nexus, he was overcome by emotion, and in ecstatic language praised the splendour of the part of creation that he had studied, or—in religious phraseology—the greatness of his Creator. (1910b, pp. 74–75)

All of the qualities usually attributed to the Buddha are present in Freud's description of da Vinci: the control of the affects, the transformation of love and hate into intellectual interest, the primacy of investigation, even the climactic ode to the greatness of his Creator. The Buddha's exclamation at the moment of his enlightenment makes these similarities all the more apparent:

I wandered through the rounds of countless births,
Seeking but not finding the builder of this house.
Sorrowful indeed is birth again and again.
Oh, housebuilder!
    You have now been seen.
You shall build the house no longer.
All your rafters have been broken,
Your ridgepole shattered.
My mind has attained to unconditional freedom.
Achieved is the end of craving.

          (Goldstein and Kornfield, 1987, p. 83)

In the Buddhist view, which emphasizes transformation rather than extinction of passion, transformation is accomplished, not by trying to eliminate troubling feelings, but by "wisely seeing them." Even in Buddhist cultures, this has always been a difficult concept to convey. When Hung-jen, the Fifth Zen Patriarch of seventh-century China, challenged his followers to compose a verse demonstrating their understanding of the Buddha's teachings, his foremost student gave an answer that reinforced the view of emotions as polluting of mind and body. Shen-hsiu presented the following verse:

The body is the Bodhi tree,
The mind is like a clear mirror standing.
Take care to wipe it all the time,
Allow no grain of dust to cling.

Shen-hsiu's verse made a virtue of the empty reflecting mind cleansed of all impurities. Today, he might be viewed by psychoanalysts as fixated in the anal stage. We can imagine him wiping his emotions away as fast as they materialize. An illiterate kitchen boy, Hui-neng (638–713), grasped the imperfection of Shen-hsiu's response and presented the following alternative:

> The Bodhi is not a tree,
> The clear mirror is nowhere standing.
> Fundamentally not one thing exists;
> Where then is a grain of dust to cling?
>
> (Merton, 1961, pp. 18–19)

Hui-neng's response avoided the trap of idealization that Shen-hsiu's poem retained. We do not need to cleanse the mind and body, he implied, we must only learn how to see properly.

As a therapist, I often have the experience of helping someone discover a difficult feeling like anger and then hearing them ask, "I don't quite understand. What should I *do* with this anger? Should I go home and get mad?" Like Shen-hsiu, we cannot help feeling that we have to eliminate the anger from our being. In today's psychological culture, we speak of *expressing* our emotions, or acting them out, but the impulse is often still to get rid of them. If we fail to do this, we feel we are somehow cheating ourselves. Once we let the feeling back in, we then feel responsible to it. Yet this is still treating the feeling as if it were an independent entity. The idea of simply *knowing* the feeling does not often occur to us.

In a situation like this, I will often respond with something like, "You don't have to *do* anything. Let it do you!"

"That's a very Zen answer," a patient recently responded. "How am I supposed to do that?"

The Buddha, of course, made this the focus of his teachings. His view was that awareness itself was the engine of sublimation; its cultivation permitted a method of working through emotions that would not have otherwise been available. In the Buddha's view, one need not condemn the instinctual emotions once they are made conscious—one must instead carefully examine the underlying feeling of identification that accompanies emotion. In making this identification the focus, the Buddhist approach pulls the rug out from under the reactive emotions, while opening up a new avenue for working them through. Shifting attention from the emotion to the *identification* with the emotion, we experience it in a new way. It is analogous to the experience of trying to see a distant star with the naked eye: by looking away from it just a bit, we actually see it more clearly.

When we meditate with the idea of getting rid of our emotions, we are actually empowering the very forces that we seek to escape. On the other hand, when we can use the arising of emotion to examine our underlying sense of identification, we tap the transformative potential of sublimation. Rather than feeling guilty every time we experience an emotion, we can use the opportunity that the emotion provides to feel our most basic identifications. Then, like Freud's da Vinci, we can find ourselves not devoid of passion but able to experience what Freud called the "persistence, constancy, and penetration which is derived from passion." The Buddha did not describe himself as one who had put his emotional life to sleep, after all. He described himself as awake.

References

Freud, S. (1910a). Five lectures on psycho-analysis. In volume 11 of *Standard Edition of the Complete Psychological Works of Sigmund Freud*, ed. and trans. James Strachey. London: Hogarth and Institute of Psychoanalysis, 1957.

Freud, S. (1910b). *Leonardo da Vinci and a Memory of His Childhood. Standard Edition*, 11.

Goldstein, J., and Kornfield, J. (1987). *Seeking the Heart of Wisdom.* Boston: Shambhala.

Merton, T. (1961). *Mystics and Zen Masters.* New York: Dell.

IX
Freud and the Psychology of Mystical Experience
(1996)

Howeover ambivalent most contemporary practitioners of transpersonal psychology may be about Freud, it is safe to say that there would be no transpersonal psychology as we know it without Freud's influence. Freud might be considered the grandfather of the entire movement. His relationship to the field is analogous to his relationship to the psychology of women: Just as Freud pioneered the study of women's psychology but remained confused about essential aspects of it, so too did he pioneer the study of spirituality while remaining confused about its place in a healthy psyche. Although he took stands in such works as *Moses and Monotheism* and *The Future of an Illusion* that were judgmental of spiritual experience, he was deeply interested in the subject and made great contributions to it. He taught, nurtured, fought with, anticipated, and influenced most of the pioneers in the field, such as Carl Jung. Despite his involvement in trying to solve the mysteries inherent in the subject, he was blind to certain fundamental aspects of it. The transpersonal field is still trying to sort out where Freud's contributions begin and where his misunderstandings end.

Freud's contributions can be grouped into three categories. First, his descriptions of the oceanic feeling as the apotheosis of the religious experience have influenced the ways in which generations of psychotherapists have interpreted spirituality. His equation of this oceanic feeling with the bliss of primary narcissism, the unambivalent union of infant and mother at the breast, has served as the gold standard for psychological explanations of meditative or mystical attainments. Second, his exploration of voluntary manipulations of attention—first in hypnosis, then in free association, and finally in evenly suspended attention—prefigured later interest on the part of the therapeutic community in meditation and sensory awareness. Freud's efforts were pioneering from a transpersonal perspective in that they opened up awareness as a therapeutic tool. Third, some of Freud's most important conceptual contributions—of the pleasure principle as the source of suffering in life and his ideas of going beyond it through sublimation—echo the teachings of the Buddha and prefigure transpersonal themes.

Far from the supreme rationalist that Freud sometimes wished he could be, Freud was constantly sifting myth, dreams, religious experience, sex, and emotion for truths about the human psyche. He was consistently amazed at the unpredictable power of the human mind and entertained his analytic colleagues with stories of inexplicable psychic or telepathic phenomena that he had witnessed in his consulting room. He corresponded with a wide range of figures, some of whom were more open to mystical experiences than he was, and he always attempted to understand their experiences from the perspective of his developing theories.

The Oceanic Feeling

One of Freud's more mystically inclined friends and correspondents was the French poet Romain Rolland, who had become a devout follower of the Hindu gurus Ramakrishna and Vivekananda. In attempting to understand Rolland's meditative experiences, Freud put forward his own explanations in his volume of 1930 entitled *Civilization and Its Discontents*. Rolland began corresponding with Freud in 1927 shortly after the publication of Freud's *The Future of an Illusion*. As Freud described the exchange:

> I had sent him my small book that treats religion as an illusion, and he answered that he entirely agreed with my judgement upon religion, but that he was sorry I had not properly appreciated the true source of religious sentiments. This, he says, consists in a peculiar feeling, which he himself is never without, which he finds confirmed by many others, and which he may suppose is present in millions of people. It is a feeling which he would like to call a sensation of 'eternity,' a feeling as of something limitless, unbounded—as it were, 'oceanic.' This feeling, he adds, is a purely subjective fact, not an article of faith; it brings with it no assurance of personal immortality, but it is the source of the religious energy which is seized upon by the various Churches and

> religious systems, directed by them into particular
> channels, and doubtless also exhausted by them
> (Freud, 1930, p. 64)

Freud took Rolland's description very seriously; it puzzled and intrigued him that he (Freud) was able to grasp the subjective quality of the feeling described without finding it in his own experience. As Freud described it, Rolland's views "caused me no small difficulty. I cannot discover this 'oceanic' feeling in myself" (1930, p. 65). Rolland's views proved something of a koan for Freud.[1] As he mused on their meaning, he began to explore the issue of ego boundaries and their relationship to mystical experience in a manner that prefigures much of transpersonal psychology.

"Normally," suggested Freud, "there is nothing of which we are more certain than the feeling of our self, of our own ego. This ego appears to us as something autonomous and unitary, marked off distinctly from everything else" (p. 66). Echoing the Buddhist psychologists of whom he was altogether ignorant, Freud went on to question this view of an independent, autonomous ego. "Such an appearance is deceptive" (p. 66), suggested Freud, because the ego continues inwardly with no clear boundary into the unconscious entity that he named the id. He termed the ego a "kind of facade" that surrounds and obscures the unconscious but that is not really separate from it. Thus Freud used his psychoanalytic explorations to break down the intrinsic certainty of most people in the ego's inviolability, but he emphasized the *internal* direction of the ego's infinitude. For Freud, the ego was but a tiny part of an infinite unconscious that continued forever inwardly.

Yet Freud recognized that this lack of boundary with the

id was not the source of Rolland's feeling of eternity. Rolland suggested a connection to the *external* world, a feeling of merger or oneness with all of creation, not a sense of the infinite depth of the unconscious. This was the state that Freud could not readily find in his own experience.

"Towards the outside," Freud suggested, "the ego seems to maintain clear and sharp lines of demarcation. There is only one state—admittedly an unusual state, but not one that can be stigmatized as pathological—in which it does not do this" (p. 66). Only in the state of being in love, decided Freud, does the boundary between ego and the external world melt away. "Against all the evidence of his senses, a man who is in love declares that 'I' and 'you' are one, and is prepared to behave as if it were a fact" (p. 66). Taking this capacity of the ego to dissolve into another, Freud went back to the experience of the infant at the breast and suggested that there once existed a state of merger that predated the emergence of the self-conscious ego in which the infant was essentially dissolved in love. Freud deduced that

> originally, the ego includes everything, . . . later it separates off an external world from itself. Our present ego-feeling is, therefore, only a shrunken residue of a much more inclusive—indeed, an all-embracing—feeling which corresponded to a more intimate bond between the ego and the world around it. (p. 68)

Rolland's experience must have resurrected this original ego feeling, Freud decided, returning him to a state reminiscent of that of the infant at the breast whose ego contained everything. He supported his argument by referring to another, unnamed friend, who had made "the most unusual experiments" with yoga and had induced regressions to "primordial states of mind" (p. 72).

On the basis of a limited knowledge of the meditation traditions of the East, therefore, Freud came to a conception of the individual ego as extending infinitely in both internal and external directions. Each individual, he hypothesized, contains the entire universe, because each ego extends infinitely to encompass both the inner unconscious and the external world. After his correspondence with Rolland, he decided that mystical experiences had the capacity to return someone to the state of merger with the external world that characterized the infantile state. Yet Freud was apparently not entirely satisfied with this formulation; in his final recorded entry in his collected works, written in 1938, Freud was still struggling with this question. In this entry, Freud wrote of mysticism as a route to exploring the *internal* dimension of the psyche. "Mysticism is the obscure self-perception of the realm outside the ego, of the id" (p. 300), he wrote just before his death, redirecting our attention once again from the external back to the depths of the psyche.

Freud's attempts to understand spiritual experiences are typical of psychologists both in and out of the transpersonal field. His recognition of the similarity between certain mystical experiences and early infantile experiences of unconditional love cannot simply be dismissed as reductionistic. Because the two experiences *are* similar, such mystical states can be tremendously reassuring for those with deficits in their early experiences of intimacy. Although most psychoanalysts have followed Freud's lead in seeing mystical experience in this way, transpersonal theorists have tended to ignore the ways in which mystical experiences of unity evoke primitive narcissistic cravings, focusing instead on the expansive or transcendent nature of those states. The expansive nature of the oceanic experience can clearly invigorate the self, but such states also provide the opportunity to work through early narcissistic issues in a new way. The spiritual path is ultimately about confronting one's own inherent narcissism, after all is said and done. Freud laid the foundation, however incomplete, for this understanding.

Evenly Suspended Attention

Freud's major breakthrough, which he referred to over and over again in his writings, was his discovery that it is possible to suspend what he called the "critical faculty" of the thinking mind. This suspension was what made the practice of psychoanalysis possible for Freud. It was the key to both the free association of the patient and the evenly suspended attention of the therapist. It is a feat that Freud apparently taught himself without knowing that this was precisely the attentional stance that Eastern meditators had been invoking for millennia.

Freud's writings on the subject reveal the most essential quality of evenly suspended attention: its impartiality. Repeatedly admonishing psychoanalysts to "suspend . . . judgement and give . . . impartial attention to everything there is to observe" (1909, p. 23), Freud insisted that in this state it was possible to understand phenomena of the mind in a unique fashion. Remaining interested in psychic content, he nevertheless encouraged his followers to practice a kind of beginning meditation while listening to their patients. His instructions have all the clarity of the writings of the best Buddhist teachers. In his definitive article on the subject, Freud (1912) can be appreciated in his best Zen-like form:

The rule for the doctor may be expressed: 'He should withhold all conscious influences from his capacity to attend, and give himself over completely to his "unconscious memory." ' Or, to put it purely in terms of technique: 'He should simply listen, and not bother about whether he is keeping anything in mind.' (pp. 111–112)

Freud's credo that the therapist should "simply listen, and not bother about whether he is keeping anything in mind" led him to some rather remarkable conclusions. He became convinced of a kind of unconscious, or psychic, communication between therapist and patient that he felt was the most important therapeutic tool that the therapist could offer:

Experience soon showed that the attitude which the analytic physician could most advantageously adopt was to surrender himself to his own unconscious mental activity, in a state of *evenly suspended attention,* to avoid so far as possible reflection and the construction of conscious expectations, not to try to fix anything that he heard particularly in his memory, and by these means to catch the drift of the patient's unconscious with his own unconscious. (1923, p. 239)

As explicit as Freud was about the critical importance of evenly suspended attention, therapists have had great difficulty in practicing his advice and overcoming the tendency to relate to patients cognitively. Otto Fenichel (1941) dismissed the efforts of those who struggled to implement Freud's original recommendations by accusing them of merely floating in their unconscious and of doing "hardly any work at all" (p. 5).

What analysts such as Fenichel failed to understand is that it is possible for a single conscious state of mind—a poised and balanced state of bare, or evenly suspended, attention—to encompass both nonverbal and rational, intellectual thought. This does not have to be an unconscious process, as Freud seemed to imply. This is one area in which transpersonal psychology may be able to give something back to psychoanalysis. The cognitive processing that Fenichel and many psychoanalysts regard so highly does not have to be sought after by the therapist; there is more than enough of it happening of its own accord. When there is something meaningful to say, it is more than apparent. More often than not, however, the intellectual activity of the therapist is a defense against experiencing the patient's being, a refusal to enter the jointly experienced not-knowing that makes discovery a real possibility.

Although Freud's picture of the state of evenly suspended attention aptly describes the meditative stance, he emphasized only the value for the therapist in catching the drift of the patient's unconscious. What he did not describe is the impact of this state of mind on the patient. The state that Freud described is necessary not just because it offers the possibility of unconscious transmission, but also because it is only in this state that the therapist's mind is not felt as an intrusion by the patient. The therapist's expectations and desires, however subtle, create a pressure against which the patient is compelled to react or with which the patient is compelled to comply. The analogy with the intrusive or ignoring parent cannot be exaggerated.

Much of the emphasis of the transpersonal psychology

movement on cultivating the power of awareness has its roots not only in Eastern thought but also in Freud's pioneering experiments with therapeutic attention. Present-day therapists would not be in a position to appreciate the Eastern modes of manipulating attention were it not for Freud's pioneering efforts in that direction. To suspend the "critical faculty" is not something that most people could come to on their own, yet Freud somehow managed to create a movement based on that very phenomenon.

Beyond the Pleasure Principle

Freud's final contribution to transpersonal psychology lies in his elucidation of the pleasure principle, the cause, in his view, of much of our self-imposed misery. In his descriptions of the pleasure principle, Freud unknowingly paralleled the first two of the Buddha's Four Noble Truths, the truth of suffering and of its cause. In early life, Freud said, the state of "psychical rest" or contentment is first disturbed by the demands of internal needs for food, comfort, warmth, and so on (1911, p. 219). Whatever was needed was originally provided (by the mother) magically, "in a hallucinatory manner," giving the child a feeling of omnipotence or magical control. This feeling that every need could be immediately satisfied, every sense pleasure immediately obtained, or every unpleasurable sensation immediately avoided is the foundation of what the Buddha described as our sense of pervasive unsatisfactoriness. We crave the original feeling of pleasure but cannot realize it. Although the pleasure principle is the first organizing principle of the human psyche, its persistence, according to both the Buddha and Freud, can be the source of much emotional turmoil. As Freud described it:

It was only the non-occurrence of the expected satisfaction, the disappointment experienced, that led
to the abandonment of this attempt at satisfaction
by means of hallucination. Instead of it, the psychical apparatus had to decide to form a conception of
the real circumstances in the external world and to
endeavor to make a real alteration in them. A new
principle of mental functioning was thus introduced; what was presented in the mind was no
longer what was agreeable but what was real, even if
it happened to be disagreeable. This setting-up of
the reality principle proved to be a momentous
step. (1911, p. 219)

It was only by forsaking an exclusive reliance on the pleasure
principle, Freud taught, that the higher pleasures could be
achieved. It is paradoxical, but nevertheless true, that spiritual
experiences depend on just this acceptance of reality.

Within both transpersonal psychology and psychoanalysis, there exists a perspective on working with reality that
senses the possibility of transformation through the bringing
of awareness to the very feelings of desire and dissatisfaction
that are often feared or rejected. Although it is not often viewed
this way, this process, which Freud called *sublimation,* is another important link between psychoanalysis and spirituality.
Frustrated in our demands to make the pleasure principle
operative, we can bring nonjudgmental awareness to bear on
that very frustration and so begin the transformative process
that is crucial to both sublimation and spiritual growth.

Freud (1910a) described sublimation as the means by
which "the energy of the infantile wishful impulses is not cut
off but remains ready for use—the unserviceable aim of the

various impulses being replaced by one that is higher, and perhaps no longer sexual" (pp. 53–54). Sublimation, for Freud, held out the possibility of escape from the pleasure principle, but he did not imply that the passions themselves were inherently dangerous. In his descriptions of Leonardo da Vinci's mental state, for instance, Freud described how da Vinci was able to "throw off" the positive or negative signs of love and hate and transform them into "intellectual interest." He was not "devoid of passion," insisted Freud (1910b). "He had merely converted his passion into a thirst for knowledge.... At the climax of a discovery" (pp. 74–75), said Freud, da Vinci's emotion would come rushing forth in a kind of ecstasy.

Freud provided an alternative model in these writings for the mystical experience. It need not be a regression to infantile omnipotence or to the demands of the pleasure principle but could, instead, grow out of the relentless pursuit of knowledge and self-awareness that he attributed to da Vinci. By throwing off the positive and negative signs of love and hate, Freud proposed, by not grasping after the pleasant and rejecting the unpleasant, one could come to an ecstatic experience of mystical proportions. For all of his antipathy toward religion, Freud came to a place of tremendous spiritual resonance.

Note

1. A *koan* is a riddle designed to paralyze the rational, thinking mind, used in Zen meditation.

References

Fenichel, O. (1941). *Problems of Psychoanalytic Technique.* New York: Psycho-analytic Quarterly.

Freud, S. (1909). Analysis of a phobia in a five-year-old boy. In volume 10 of

Standard Edition of the Complete Psychological Works of Sigmund Freud, ed. and trans. James Strachey. London: Hogarth and Institute of Psycho-analysis, 1955.

—— (1910a). Five lectures on psycho-analysis. *Standard Edition.* 11, 1957.

—— (1910b). Leonardo da Vinci and a memory of his childhood. *Standard Edition.* 11, 1957.

—— (1911). Formulations on the two principles of mental functioning. *Standard Edition.* 12, 1958.

—— (1912). Recommendations to physicians practicing psychoanalysis. *Standard Edition.* 12, 1958.

—— (1923). Two encyclopedia articles. *Standard Edition.* 18, 1955.

—— (1930). Civilization and its discontents. *Standard Edition.* 21, 1961.

—— (1938/1941). Findings, ideas, problems. *Standard Edition.* 23, 1964.

PART THREE

Winnicott

After the publication of "Beyond the Oceanic Feeling" in *The International Review of Psycho-Analysis*, I received several letters from local psychoanalysts asking to make my acquaintance. One was from a psychiatrist named Emmanuel Ghent, who lived close by in a loft in Soho. Ghent was an analyst who had taken twenty years off from analytic work to compose electronic music for Bell Labs, but who was now involved in the relational track of NYU's postdoctoral program in psychotherapy and psychoanalysis. He asked me if I had read a new book by Adam Phillips called *Winnicott*. I had not. Another letter came from a psychoanalyst named Michael Eigen, who also sent along a copy of his book *The Psychotic Core*, where, among many eye-opening passages, I found a beautiful and evocative summary of Winnicott's views on unintegration and unknowing. While I knew of Winnicott, I did not yet appreciate him. Ghent and Eigen took me by the hand and led me to him, providing me with a bridge between Freud and Buddha, introducing me to a man whose writings anticipated the convergence of the two.

These final four chapters all bear the imprint of Winnicott, whose ideas I use to show how easily the psychoanalytic and Buddhist worlds can relate. Chapters 10 and 13 are inspired by Winnicott's theories of creativity and use contemporary art as an intermediary between Buddhism and psychoanalysis. Underlying these works is a view of psychotherapy as a creative endeavor. If it had not already become something of a cliché, I might have titled one of them "Zen and the Art of Therapy." Chapter 11, written in honor of Emmanuel Ghent after his passing, contains the essential ideas that were to later appear in my book *Open to Desire*, which treats desire as a worthy subject of meditation, not, as is so often the case, as an impediment to spiritual growth. Chapter 12, "The Structure of No Structure," describes the relationship of Winnicott's ideas of unintegration to the Buddhist notion of no-self. Mindful of how difficult it can be to cogently convey the Buddha's insights into the nature of self, I am grateful for Winnicott's musings. They help to give the flavor of the Buddha's psychology while speaking in the language of the twenty-first century. The Buddha, it is said, was reluctant at first to even speak of his realizations, fearing that no one would understand him. "That will be wearisome to me," he remarked, "that will be tiresome to me." He was finally convinced that there were some people in the world, with but "little dust in their eyes," able to grasp that the self was not an absolute reality. As the Buddha's ideas have taken root in cultures throughout the world, it is always because a few people are ready to consider this notion. Winnicott was one such clear-eyed individual.

X
Sip My Ocean
Emptiness as Inspiration
(2004)

There are a few men from whom their contemporaries do not withhold admiration, although their greatness rests on attributes and achievements which are completely foreign to the aims and ideals of the multitude. . . . One of these exceptional few calls himself my friend in his letters to me. I had sent him my small book that treats religion as an illusion, and he answered that he entirely agreed with my judgment upon religion, but that he was sorry I had not properly appreciated the true source of religious sentiments. This, he says, consists in a peculiar feeling, which he himself is never without, which he finds confirmed by many others, and which he may suppose is present in millions of people. It is a feeling which he would like

to call a sensation of 'eternity,' a feeling as of something limitless,
unbounded—as it were 'oceanic.' . . .
The views expressed by the friend whom I so honor, and who
himself once praised the magic of illusion in a poem, caused me
no small difficulty. I cannot discover this 'oceanic' feeling in
myself. It is not easy to deal scientifically with feelings.
    —*Sigmund Freud,* Civilization and Its Discontents

I n talking about the meeting points of Buddhism, psychotherapy, and contemporary art, I mean this chapter to complement other discussions (Tucker, 2004) about how the breakdown of the art object as "entity" in the late 1960s and early 1970s was mirrored and supported by Buddhist notions of egolessness and interdependence, ideas that were also breaking into Western culture during those years. Because the primary conceptual tenet of Buddhism is the lack of a central essence or substance to the self, Buddhism provided a natural inspiration to—or confirmation for—artists in the process of discovering how exciting art could become when freed from the restraints of materialism. Before postmodern notions of the spuriousness of self or the relativity of the object, it turns out, there was Buddhism. Listen to the Italian writer Roberto Calasso (1998) as he speaks of this relationship between the ancient and the modern, between East and West.

> What would one day be called "the modern" was, at
> least as far as its sharpest and most hidden point is
> concerned, a legacy of the Buddha. Seeing things as

so many aggregates and dismantling them. Then dismantling the elements split off from the aggregates, insofar as they too are aggregates. And so on and on in dizzying succession. An arid, ferocious scholasticism. A taste for repetition, as agent provocateur of inanity. Vocation for monotony. Total lack of respect for any prohibition, any authority. Emptying of every substance from within. Only husks left intact. The quiet conviction that all play occurs where phantoms ceaselessly substitute one for another. Allowing the natural algebra of the mind to operate out in the open. Seeing the world as a landscape of interlocking cogs. Observing it from a certain and constant distance. But what distance exactly? No question could be more contentious. Adding this last doubt, then, to a trail of other gnawing uncertainties. (p. 368)

Calasso gets it exactly. The phenomenology of the classical Buddhist psychology known as Abhidhamma was a precursor to modernism's atomization of reality. Conceptually, Buddhism and modernism are of a piece. Analytically breaking down the edifice of objective reality so that an underlying sheer ephemerality is revealed. Dematerializing the object, be it the artwork or the self. Pulling the viewer from the safety of his or her observing stance into the mix of interdependent relativity, like the Paul McCarthy piece we once stumbled into, where my wife and daughter found themselves suddenly donning a Pinocchio costume while being pulled inextricably into the artwork. The observer and that which is observed are both part of an interpenetrating reality, and what we do with our attention determines how we experience that reality.

These are discoveries that have been mirrored in the psychotherapy world over the past thirty years, where the safety of the therapist's neutral and observing stance has given way to a new theory of "intersubjectivity" or "relationality," where the interest of the therapist is no longer in the separate self of the patient but in the relational field that exists between therapist and client. Even in the last bastion of selfhood, the world of psychotherapy, the territory of the individual ego has had to give way.

But Buddhism offers something more than an analytical breakdown of objective reality. It has a process, conveyed through meditation, that affirms something essential about the making, and experiencing, of art. Buddhism, in its rejection of ritual, ceremony, sacrifice, and community obligation —in its renunciation of memory, desire, and the primacy of conceptual organization—drove its practitioners deeper and deeper into themselves, affirming (at the same time as it challenged) their subjectivity and individuality. The questioning of the self as object did not leave Buddhists floating in a boundaryless cosmic ooze. Even as it stripped away identity, Buddhist meditation affirmed a reservoir of self (a selfless reservoir) that is intensely private, and potentially very creative. It is this aspect that I would like to dwell upon.

As Calasso points out, in Buddhism the central attentional strategy, at least at the beginning, is to observe from a certain, constant, and hard-to-define distance. Tibetan Buddhists describe it as a setting up of a "spy-consciousness" that observes everything as if from a corner of the mind. This is a mental stance, or posture, that underlies all of Buddhism's vast teachings. From the monastic practices of the Theravada cultures of Southeast Asia (the closest that we have to the original Buddhism of the Buddha's time of 500 BC) to the Ch'an and

Zen practices of China and Japan (where Buddhism merged with the prevailing Taoist ideologies of harmony with nature) to the more esoteric Vajrayana practices of Tibet (where the Tantric Buddhism of medieval India took refuge from the destruction brought upon it by the invasion of conquering armies), this stance runs through all the different forms.

Sometimes called "bare," or naked, attention, this strategy is defined as the "clear and single-minded awareness of what actually happens *to* us and *in* us, at the successive moments of perception" (Thera, 1962, p. 30). It is different from our usual modes of perception in that it is detached and receptive, allowing for an exact registering of whatever is happening in the mind and body, carefully separating our mental or emotional reactions from the core events themselves. Sometimes called mindfulness, or moment-to-moment awareness, bare attention is the sine qua non of meditation, the distinctive contribution of the Buddha's approach. It might be described as a kind of radical acceptance of, or tolerance for, all of our experience.

There is a Japanese haiku that expresses this mental posture perfectly. Many of you may be familiar with it. It goes like this:

The old pond.
A frog jumps in.
Plop!

The old pond is your mind, which you are watching in meditation, in a state similar to that which psychoanalysts have recognized requires a therapeutic split in the ego. Detached and receptive, you observe your own mind without judgments. Quiet or noisy, windswept or still, beautiful or not: an old pond. *A frog jumps in.* Something happens. A thought or a feeling courses through you. You have a memory of someone hurting your feelings; a disappointment. Or a new idea excites you. *Plop.* Reverberations. Your mind goes on and on about it. One thing leads to another. Maybe you get involved emotionally. Disappointment is linked to frustration. Anger bubbles up. Muscles stiffen, the breath gets shallow. But you are still watching the pond, allowing the reactions but noticing how distinct they are from the core event, how they alternate between pleasant and unpleasant, how they flow into each other, and how they are simultaneously you and not you. You are both watching and being watched, or is that even correct? Maybe there is only: *Plop.*

The state of bare attention is not an unfamiliar one to the artist. Many with whom I have worked or spoken recognize something of their studio selves in the descriptions that come from Buddhist teachers. The combination of focused concentration and open, nondiscriminating awareness is one that many artists find essential for the creative process. Not that they do not also make judgments and comparisons; think, plan or evaluate; or strategize about how their works fit into various competing ideologies. But there is something in the internal dynamics of the creative process that thrives on this kind of attention. It is a state in which new ideas present themselves, in which old ideas loosen their grip, in which the force of habit can be seen for what it is. *Plop.*

This is also a state of mind that is not unfamiliar to the psychotherapist. When Freud (1909) gave instructions to physicians practicing psychoanalysis, he used to tell them to "suspend . . . judgment and give impartial attention to everything there is to observe" (p. 23). Freud suggested an optimal state of mind that was characterized by two fundamental properties:

the absence of reason or deliberate attempts to select, concentrate, or understand; and even, equal, and impartial attention to all that occurs in the field of awareness. This technique, said Freud (1912),

> is a very simple one. As we shall see, it rejects the use of any special expedient (even that of taking notes). It consists simply in not directing one's notice to anything in particular and in maintaining the same 'evenly-suspended attention' (as I have called it) in the face of all that one hears. . . . It will be seen that the rule of giving equal notice to everything is the necessary counterpart to the demand made on the patient that he should communicate everything that occurs to him without criticism or selection. If the doctor behaves otherwise, he is throwing away most of the advantage which results from the patient's obeying the 'fundamental rule of psychoanalysis.' The rule for the doctor may be expressed: 'He should withhold all conscious influences from his capacity to attend, and give himself over completely to his "unconscious memory".' Or to put it purely in terms of technique: 'He should simply listen, and not bother about whether he is keeping anything in mind.' (pp. 111–112)

James Joyce talked about something similar when he described the best way to look at a work of art. He used the word "beholding," but I think he was describing something of what Freud was pointing to when he suggested that we "catch the drift" of someone's unconscious with our own. If you pull the artwork toward you, the experience becomes pornographic,

Joyce said, but if you distance yourself too much, it becomes criticism. The correct approach requires some sort of middle ground, where the viewer surrenders himself to his own unconscious experience of the object.

Another, more contemporary psychoanalyst, Christopher Bollas (1987), refers to this as an "aesthetic moment." The aesthetic moment involves a "subjective rapport" in which "the subject feels held in symmetry and solitude by the spirit of the object" (p. 16). These are "fundamentally wordless occasions," Bollas insists, "a moment of sudden awe . . . a suspended moment when self and object feel reciprocally enhancing and mutually informative" (p. 31). What Bollas implies, but does not formulate explicitly, is that subject and object lose their entitativeness under the spell of such moments. Some might call it a loss of boundaries, but, alternatively, we might see such times as the opening of a window on the mind that underlies our usual worlds of self and other.

The best recent exponent of bare attention was the composer and artist John Cage, whose music and art essentially became a pure expression of this mental posture. Cage's descriptions of his process do much to make the links between art, psychology, and Buddhism understandable. "If you develop an ear for sounds that are musical it is like developing an ego," said Cage. "You begin to refuse sounds that are not musical and that way cut yourself off from a good deal of experience. . . . The most recent change in my attitude toward sound has been in relation to loud sustained sounds such as car alarms or burglar alarms, which used to annoy me, but which I now accept and even enjoy. I think the transformation came through a statement of Marcel Duchamp who said that sounds which stay in one location and don't change can produce a sonorous sculpture, a sound sculpture that lasts in time. Isn't that beautiful?" (Nisker, 1986, p. 4).

In talking about the interrelationship of art, psychotherapy, and Buddhism, it is clear that all three disciplines thrive when the curious, in-between, state of bare attention is allowed to become dominant. Much of the excitement about Buddhism in both therapeutic and art-making circles has to do with this fact. Both artists and psychoanalysts have had to find their own path into this state—Buddhism knows, and can teach, the way, and has some important things to say about what to do when you get there.

But it is in the world of psychoanalysis, most specifically in the work of the British child analyst D. W. Winnicott, that I have found the most cogent descriptions of what is actually happening in meditation and why it is relevant to cultural, or artistic, expression. Winnicott was a master of the in-between, of transitional space, of formless experience, intermediate areas, and the worlds between that of inner life and relationships with other people. In many different ways, he spoke about "bridges to be kept open between the imagination and everyday existence" (Winnicott, 1965, p. 187). He was interested in playing, creativity, spontaneity, and intimacy, but also in those areas of psychic life that are private, uncommunicable, still, silent, and intensely personal. "The written words of psychoanalysis do not seem to tell us all that we want to know," he wrote. "What, for instance, are we doing when we are listening to a Beethoven symphony or making a pilgrimage to a picture gallery or reading *Troilus and Cressida* in bed, or playing tennis? What is a child doing when sitting on the floor playing with toys under the aegis of the mother? What is a group of teenagers doing participating in a pop session? It is not only: what are we doing? The question also needs to be posed: where are we (if anywhere at all)? We have used the concepts of inner and outer, and we want a third concept. Where are we when we are doing what in fact we do a great deal of our time, namely, enjoying ourselves?" (Winnicott, 1971, pp. 105–106).

Winnicott is relevant because he was not afraid to point to this third place—that which is neither inner nor outer—and to link it to play, creativity, and spirituality. While he did not use the language of Buddhism or of meditation, he did describe the space that bare attention evokes. Because he rooted all of his discussions in the experiences of childhood, he made clear something that Buddhism, in its own way, also stresses: the state of bare attention is natural to us. It may have been forgotten, or it may be in hiding—it may even feel threatening for one reason or another—but it is natural to our being. Discovering it always involves a sense of recovery. Art-making, in its own way, also requires touching this space—and part of our veneration of the art-object, or the art-viewing experience, is due to the way it evokes a similar state in the viewer. "Theater takes place all the time, wherever one is," said John Cage, "and art simply facilitates persuading one that this is the case" (Nisker, 1986, p. 4). Art is another portal into the space of bare attention.

As Buddhists have dissected their worldly experience, they have, as Roberto Calasso made clear, dismantled the elements of subjective and objective realities into so many aggregates. Like modern physicists, or modern artists, they have taken apart the conventional view of things and forced us to rethink the way things actually are. In so doing, they have come to a clearer and clearer understanding of how imprisoning our notions of inner and outer, of self and object, can be.

Because nothing can be found that exists in its own right, because nothing can be seen to have inherent existence or a persisting individual nature, everything is seen to be dependent on everything else, and therefore relative.

This vision of an interpenetrating relativity is related to the one that Winnicott had when describing what happens between mother and infant. As mother and child begin to separate out from one another, what he called a "potential space" begins to open up between them. The baby's trust in the mother's reliability allows that space to be experienced, and filled with "creative playing, with the use of symbols, and with all that eventually adds up to a cultural life" (Winnicott, 1971, p. 109). Trust in the mother allows the baby to experience the potential space, and experiencing it permits play. In much the same way in meditation, trust in bare attention allows the full experience of the mind, which permits the play of the world—John Cage's theater—to be appreciated.

It is important to understand that in Buddhism one great mistake is warned about time and again. Understanding of emptiness, or *sunyata*, does not permit reification of nothingness. In opening up access to the third space of intermediate experience, Buddhism asserts that there is something positive, something joyful, something creative, that underlies all experience. While the self, or the object, may not be the concrete, self-sufficient entity that we imagined, the alternative is not nothingness. Emptiness is best compared to the hollow of a pregnant womb; it is derived from the Sanskrit word *svi*, which means swelling, like the swelling of a seed as it expands. There is a fullness to Buddhist emptiness, a sense of spaciousness that both holds and suffuses the stuff of the world. Not to appreciate this fullness is the great stumbling block of the deconstruction of the self, and one that many people, including some contemporary artists, fall prey to. "Emptiness has been said to be the relinquishment of views," said the great Buddhist scholar Nagarjuna, "but those who hold to the view of emptiness are incurable" (Cleary, 1986, p. 19). The great challenge of emptiness is the ability to truly appreciate the stuff of this world, qualified, as it is said in the Buddhist teachings, by "*mere* existence."

This capacity to know things as they are, qualified by mere existence, is what links the artist, the meditator, and the psychotherapist. Each opens up the possibility of bare attention and transitional space; each permits a peek at the play of emptiness that underlies conventional reality. While Buddhist art in Asia became iconic, changing little over the past six or seven hundred years after a thousand years of dynamic evolution, the emergence of a living Buddhism in our culture has generated the potential for another metamorphosis, another turning of the wheel. Rather than repeating the same forms over and over again, today's artists have the opportunity to reinterpret Buddhist insights in a contemporary context, and to express Buddhist insights in their work. They do not have to be officially "Buddhist" in order to do this, but they may be inspired by Buddhism's deep appreciation for the way creative expression links emptiness and form.

Buddhism is important to art at this moment because it both speaks to, and serves as an antidote for, the self-conscious nihilism that has become so prominent in our deconstructivist ideologies. While religion has often served as a refuge from society's materialism, Buddhism offers entry into the mind as a vehicle for reaffirming the positivity of the creative act. Far from the ironic bravado, and barely concealed shock, that informs much of the postmodern response to the breakdown of the art object and the self, Buddhism offers a gentle and penetrating wisdom that accepts the insubstantial nature of this world without denigrating it. Through its doctrine of emptiness, Buddhism affirms the primacy of the potential space in which the creative act occurs. It understands, in a way that our own culture has trouble finding words for, the leap of faith that art-making entails, and it believes in the process. The old pond does not lose its appeal, even if we watch it for a very long time.

Whether she intended it this way or not I do not know, but I was given a vision of this not so long ago when viewing a piece by the artist Pipilotti Rist at the Museum of Contemporary Art in Chicago entitled *Sip My Ocean*. It is a video, vaguely MTV-like—with a haunting, minimalist vocal score—of a churning ocean of changing visual forms. Alone in the viewing room, I was pulled into something of a meditative state by the unfolding work. The ocean, the unconscious, the "incommunicado self" out of which symbols arise, the potential space of the intermediate area between self and other, were all wordlessly evoked. I felt that the artist was communicating something of the creative play of emptiness that I recognized from my meditation experiences. In the midst of my reflections, I noticed something inexplicable that I have felt in similar moments of meditation: a sweetness, or joy, that seems to come from nowhere.

The taste of *mere* existence, I thought to myself, and also the flavor of art.

References

Bollas, C. (1987). *The Shadow of the Object: Psychoanalysis of the Unthought Known*. New York: Columbia University Press.

Calasso, R. (1998). *Ka: Stories of the Mind and Gods of India*. New York: Vintage.

Cleary, T. (1986). *Shobogenzo: Zen Essays by Dogen*. Honolulu: University of Hawaii Press.

Freud, S. (1909). Analysis of a phobia in a five-year-old-boy. *Standard Edition*. London: Hogarth Press, 1955, *10*, 3–152.

Freud, S. (1912). Recommendations to physicians practicing psychoanalysis. *Standard Edition*. London: Hogarth Press, 1955, *12*: 109–120.

Nisker, W. (1986). John Cage and the music of sound. *Inquiring Mind* 3, no. 2: 4–5.

Thera, N. (1962). *The Heart of Buddhist Meditation*. New York: Samuel Weiser.

Tucker, M. (2004). No title. In J. Baas & M. J. Jacob (editors), *Buddha Mind in Contemporary Art*. Berkeley: University of California Press, 2004, pp. 75–86.

Winnicott, D. W. (1965). Communicating and not communicating leading to a study of certain opposites. In *The Maturational Processes and the Facilitating Environment*. New York: International Universities Press.

Winnicott, D. W. (1971). *Playing and Reality*. London & New York: Routledge.

XI

A Strange Beauty
Emmanuel Ghent and the Psychologies of East and West
(2005)

Several years ago, before Mannie Ghent passed away, I went to a talk in lower Manhattan by an old friend and teacher of mine, a former Harvard University psychologist named Richard Alpert, now known as Ram Dass. Ram Dass has a way of blending the insights of Eastern and Western psychology that I have always admired, a quality that Mannie also shared. In his talk that evening, he touched on one of the cornerstones of his own particular synthesis of East and West, the need to move between different levels of psychic reality. Despite the ravages of a recent stroke that had temporarily robbed him of his ability to speak clearly, he sketched a version of a presentation I had heard many times over the years of our acquaintance.

"We all exist at many levels simultaneously," said Ram

Dass, sitting in his wheelchair at the front of the large Soho loft where the gathering took place. "We each have many levels of consciousness."

It was a stormy night and the rain was blowing against the skylights and windows, giving the evening a rather eerie atmosphere.

"Level number one is the ego. It has to be number one, because it's the ego." He laughed at his own joke and pounded his knee with his good arm. In his language, *ego* was a stand-in for the proud yet insecure narcissistic self, concerned, above all else, with its own preservation and gratification. "The ego is all about itself: *my* achievements, *my* needs, *my* desires. It feels itself to be an isolate in this world."

For Ram Dass, this ego was akin to D. W. Winnicott's notion of false self, that which responds to early invasiveness or abandonment by retreating to a safe mental haven where it attempts to manage the interpersonal environment that seems so threatening. The ego seeks to protect itself at the expense of others: it is an anxious place from which to operate. "A room full of egos is like a room full of trumpets, each one calling out, 'Listen to me!' With all that noise," Ram Dass continued, "we can't hear the soft melody of Krishna's flute."

Ram Dass's invocation of Krishna at this moment was telling. His Indian guru had a temple in the town of Krishna's birth. Krishna is one of the most important of the Indian gods. Stories about his childhood, youth, and adult life fill books and paintings of Indian lore. As a baby, he manifested as uninhibited eroticism that is celebrated in the Indian love of children. As a young man, he was a cowherd with a golden flute who made love simultaneously to scores of *gopis*, beautiful young women of the forest. And as an adult, he advised the warrior Arjuna in the mythic battles of the *Bhagavad Gita*, one of the holiest epics of the Hindu canon. His flute, as Ram Dass suggested, makes the sound of the divine. In India, the longing that is stimulated by the sound of that flute, or even by the idea of the sound of the flute, is itself a meditation, a form of devotional yoga called *bhakti*. As the self surrenders to that longing, a person can experience himself or herself on a different level, as a soul calling out to God.

If the first level in Ram Dass's formulation is the ego, the second level is the soul. For him, as for many steeped in Indian philosophy, the soul is that which precedes and outlasts the self of the immediate incarnation: that which is beyond the everyday concerns of the personality. But this belief in reincarnation is not a necessary precondition to understanding what Ram Dass meant by level number two. The word *soul* is a direct translation of the Greek word *psyche*. It also connotes what Jung called the "undiscovered self" and what Freud christened "the it." More extensive than the rational mind, expanding through the emotional body into the unconscious, it is, in Jung's (1957) words, "the only accessible source of religious experience" (p. 101). In the opinions of many, the psyche has a spiritual agenda as well as a personal one; its desire is to know God (or to know itself), although it is sometimes confused about where to look.

As Ram Dass is aware, the false self does not like to yield its authority. It fears its ultimate unreality. Jung (1957) was one of the first psychologists to recognize how damaging its need for control can be. "It seems a positive menace to the ego that its monarchy can be doubted," he wrote. "The religious person, on the other hand, is accustomed to the thought of not being sole master in his own house" (pp. 98–99). This is an idea that Winnicott developed in his notion of the incommunicado element and that Mannie further elaborated in his seminal paper on surrender. They each described a need to reach into a private and personal emotional world that is beyond conventional knowledge or understanding, beyond the domain of the false self, into territory that has traditionally been the province of ascetics or mystics engaged in the process of meditation. Therapeutic interest in what Winnicott meant by the incommunicado element has brought with it an investigation of early childhood preverbal experience (which Christopher Bollas [1987] has called the "unthought known"), because so much of it takes place at a level of psychic organization having nothing to do with language. But it is a mistake to see the opening to this level solely as a regression to primordial states of consciousness. This realm is present in our own lives, in our passions, our dreams, our longings, and our emotions, and opening to it as an adult is very different from regressing to an infantile experience of it. Extending deeply into the personal experience of being a separate individual is an infinite world that we can never know completely, but that nevertheless beckons us, as if from afar. To call it religious is to expand the conventional notion of spirituality, but to deny its spiritual nature is to denude the psyche unnecessarily.

This is exactly what Ram Dass took such delight in explaining. The ego is reluctant to admit an alternative to its primacy. But if it can be tricked into letting go, a vast universe opens to it. Fantasies, emotions, impulses, and dreams become windows into the unknown, bridges between the ego and the psyche. And they have the power of alerting us to the most mysterious level of all, which Ram Dass delicately referred to as "level number three," the presence of an overarching and impersonal awareness or consciousness, a mystery that continues to bedevil philosophers and neurobiologists alike.

In illustrating the third level, Ram Dass took off from

Jung's thought and brought it back home to a place that Mannie, with his understanding of playing and creative activity, would have appreciated. Ram Dass told a story of an elderly woman who came to one of his early talks when he was just back from India still garbed in psychedelic regalia. He remembered outlining a similar hierarchy of levels of psychic reality. She was dressed in a conservative manner yet sat in the front row nodding in agreement as he spoke. In his mind, she did not belong in his audience, yet she seemed totally in tune with everything he said. At the end of the evening he approached her and asked simply, but incredulously, "How do you know?" He could sense that she understood not just the ego and soul concepts but also something of the third level, what some would call God or cosmic consciousness or (in philosophies such as Buddhism in which the idea of God is deemed superfluous): Buddha-nature, "suchness," or emptiness.

"I crochet," she replied. She said nothing else.

I always think that Mannie was like that woman: not so conservative in appearance, perhaps, but with an intuitive understanding of the greatest mysteries that we face and an ease, humility, lightness, and humor that lit up his being, at every level. He *knew* things, not just from his experience as an analyst, but also from his music.

An Integrated Vision

I first met Mannie after I published an article in the *International Review of Psycho-Analysis* on Buddhism and psychotherapy. It was around 1990, and this article was the synthesis of my thinking up to that point. Mannie called me and said that he would like to meet me. It turned out that he lived only a few blocks away—and I went to his loft one afternoon and sat and talked with him while he ate apples. He probably ate five or six apples while we talked: he made a vague reference to a heart condition that had him watching his diet closely. Our conversation ranged over his history: psychiatric residency in Montreal, studies with the Italian Roberto Assagioli, time in India with Bhagwan Rajneesh before he was Rajneesh (when he was spinning an enticing blend of Western psychotherapy and Indian mysticism to mostly German devotees), 20 years composing music for Bell Labs, Philip Glass as his plumber, and the founding of the relational track of psychoanalysis at NYU. Mannie was interested in Buddhism and in my path, and he became my friend. He also pointed me, gently, to the work of D. W. Winnicott and Adam Phillips by recommending that I read Phillips's recently published *Winnicott.*

By turning me in this direction, Mannie helped to resolve an issue that had been nagging at me: the issue of desire.[1] I knew from my own experience that the sensual and the spiritual were linked in a manner implied by Ram Dass in his discussion of level number two. My early experiences of meditation had thrilled me in the same way that certain erotic relationships had, yet many in the spiritual circles of which I was a part preferred to keep the two worlds separate. There was a tendency to accept the prevailing notion that desire is the cause of human suffering, as a cursory read of the Buddha's famous Four Noble Truths might suggest, and to withdraw from any overt expression of personal agency. I preferred the more literal translation of clinging or craving as the cause of suffering, yet I had not yet found a way to explain my thinking satisfactorily. Looking to psychoanalysis for a more sympathetic understanding of the spiritual potential of desire, I found, at least at first, a much more thorough discussion of anger. Even in Ram Dass's formulation, I perceived the remnants of a hierarchical tendency, common in both psycho-analysis and in spiritual circles, to situate personal desire on the low end of a continuum that moves, through sublimation and maturing object relations, toward the sublime.

Though we have all kinds of assumptions about what the spiritual path might look like, things are rarely the way we expect them to be. Although some continue to think that desire is supposed to be eliminated through spiritual work, it may be that a different kind of transformation is closer to the truth. Mannie understood that careful, mindful attention to personal emotional life has the potential to break down the illusions of the false self. He also understood how frightening personal desire can be for those constrained by the false self's needs. Being an expert in managing the needs of others often makes one's own needs seem superfluous. Talking to him about this while watching him eat apples was clarifying in itself. Why does it always surprise us to find spiritual masters so at home in their bodies, and in their worlds? I was grateful for his more integrated vision because it affirmed something I had been struggling to articulate, that the personal and the spiritual are reflections of one another rather than two ends of a polarity. If desire is such an intrinsic aspect of my being, it does not have to be demonized. My spiritual aspirations did not have to stop me from being myself.

The point is not a trivial one. It is not only in devotees of Eastern religions that we find the hope that desire can be eliminated once and for all. In the West, this desire for the end of desire has also been strong. Our dominant way of thinking about longing suggests that, sooner or later, we should be able to outgrow it. This view, as the noted Mexican writer Octavio Paz (1993), a former ambassador to India, has described it, is rooted in the age-old assumption of Plato that eroticism is "a vital impulse that ascends, rung by rung, to the contemplation of the highest good" (p. 19). The psychic journey, as perceived from this perspective, is one of steady and gradual purification, in which one ascends from the depths of instinctual sexuality to the heights of divine contemplation. This developmental model, in which the psyche's journey is compared to ascending a ladder or walking a path, is defined by its linearity. We envision a straight line, albeit one that stretches toward the horizon or reaches toward the heavens.

Freud's ideas of sublimation expressed this Platonic ideal perfectly. The sexual currents that fuel desire, he conjectured, can be progressively diverted into a higher calling, redirected into the pursuit of knowledge, science or art. In Freud's (1910) words, "the energy of the infantile wishful impulses is not cut off but remains ready for use—the unserviceable aim of the various impulses being replaced by one that is higher, and perhaps no longer sexual" (pp. 53–54). Freud wrote a compelling psychobiography of Leonardo da Vinci that was all about this idea, in which he extolled Leonardo's passion but affirmed that it had been completely converted into a thirst for knowledge. Leonardo was Freud's paradigm for the fully analyzed individual. Behind this idea, as Paz (1993) was correct in pointing out, was one that is common in many of the world's religions, "that of the gradual purification of the soul, which at each step moves farther and farther from sexuality until, at the summit of its ascent, it relinquishes it altogether" (p. 20).

In focusing on a hierarchical model of sublimation, Freud ignored the link between the sensuous and the sacred that certain Indian traditions have always returned to, even after they postulate a need for renunciation and asceticism. The circularity of the Indian approach was something that

Freud, and many of his contemporary descendants, could not imagine. Steeped in the linearity of the Platonic ideal, these analysts were much more comfortable with primitive, or infantile, expressions of desire than with those which flirted with the ecstatic. Mannie was different. He had been touched by India and could see the possibilities of integrating psychoanalysis and Indian thought.

In keeping the discussion exclusively on the instinctual level, Freud missed something essential about desire's nature. His vision of the human organism as "stratified, composed of primitive instincts and biology below and rationality and spirituality above" has, in the words of Stephen Mitchell (2002), "in recent decades, started to fray" (p. 65). Today's psychoanalysts are starting to describe the psyche in forms that do justice to the power of sensuality instead of disparaging it. "Erotic passion destabilizes one's sense of self" (p. 92), Mitchell wrote in the same book, which touched on the spiritual aspects of romantic love, an unusual topic for a psychoanalyst. "In the dialectic of eroticism that constitutes the strange loop of our sexuality, our journey into the otherness of the other often surprises us with unknown features of ourselves, and our exploration of our interiority, the ineffable privacy of the self, often surprises us with the presence of others" (p. 92).

Tapas and Kama

In Indian mythology, the intermingling of lower and higher, sensual and spiritual, self and other, and erotic and enlightened is much more the rule. Mannie understood this, and the influence of this perspective secretly permeates his work. Mannie would have appreciated the florid Indian story of the birth of Eros, for example, in which Brahma (the four-headed creator god) made a young woman, Aurora, of such astonishing beauty that he was stopped in his tracks by desire for her. According to the *Shiva Purana* (one of the 18 collections of ancient Sanskrit stories or myths), his creation of Aurora was the moment when erotic desire first came into being. It is described by Danielou (1984) in the following scene, redolent with Freudian imagery, yet always oriented toward the divine:

> Brahma spoke, "On seeing her, I had an involuntary erection. My heart was disturbed with conflicting desires. All my sons were in the same state. A marvelous being called Eros (kama) was born of my thought. His complexion was golden, his chest strong and solid, his nose well-formed; his thighs, buttocks and calves were rounded and muscular. . . . He gave off the odour of an elephant in rut. His eyes were like lotus petals, and he was perfumed like their stamens. His neck was a conch. His emblem was a fish. He was big, mounted on a crocodile, and armed with a bow and five arrows of flowers. His amorous glances seduced everyone. He winked at all around him. His breath was like a perfumed breeze. The feeling of love came from his whole person. On seeing him, my sons were overcome with amazement. They became agitated and restless, their minds were confused. Troubled by the ardour of love, they lost their strength of mind.
>
> Brahma then said to Kama, "In this form and with your five arrows of flowers, you can inspire de-

sire, make yourself master of men and women, and
thus perpetuate the work of creation." (pp. 160–161)

The story of Eros did not stop with his birth but went on
to describe all of the trouble that unbridled passion could
create. Yet the lesson that unfolded is very different from that of
Pandora's box. The chaos of the unconscious did not spiral out
of control. Instead, the Indian tale of Eros weaves multiple and
interlocking stories about the important relationship between
asceticism and eroticism, between introspection and relationship: lessons that are of special interest to the psychoanalyst,
lessons that Mannie made use of in his writing and his work.

In Danielou's (1984) rendition of this legend, the gods
continue the narrative:

> "Having charmed us all, Eros continued making
> fun of us until we had all lost control of our senses.
> Thus it was that we let ourselves go to look at Au-
> rora with lustful eyes. . . . " All the sages were in
> a state of erotic excitement. Implored by Virtue
> (Dharma), Shiva burst out laughing and mocked
> them, making them blush with shame. He said to
> them, "Truly, Brahma, how can you allow yourself
> to get to the point of having such feelings for your
> own daughter? It is not seemly. . . . How is it that
> your sons are all smitten with the same girl, who,
> moreover, is their own sister? This Eros must be a
> fool, and lacking in good manners, to have attacked
> you with such violence." (p. 161)

Shiva, the figure who mocked Brahma and alerted the
other gods to the unthinking abandon of Eros, is the pivotal

god in the Indian pantheon, as pervasive an influence as Krishna was later to become. Like the woman whom Ram Dass questioned at his lecture, Shiva's character also reminds me of Mannie. One might think that he must be, on the basis of the comments quoted here, some kind of puritanical figure, intent on upholding virtue, but nothing could be further from the truth. Although Shiva's skill at meditation made him the one god who was impervious to the power of Eros, he was not some holier-than-thou figure. When it was called for, Shiva's erotic capacity could be infinite, as intense as his meditations. Shiva was known for his perpetually erect phallus, his *linga* of light, which threatened to destroy the world unless united with the *yoni*, or vulva, of his lover, Parvati, the Lady of the Mountain. This made him a most interesting god. Shiva embodies the interrelationship of renunciation and desire, of asceticism and eroticism, and of destruction and passion that is an inextricable aspect of Indian thought. In this way, he also connotes a psychoanalyst such as Mannie, one who is able to see the world of the psyche in all of its complexity.

Shiva cultivated a substance called *tapas,* the heat of asceticism, something like an alternative Freudian libido, said to accumulate through the power of introspection. And although it would seem that the accumulation of tapas is the precise opposite of the indulgence of desire, it is clear from the stories of Shiva's sexual exploits that this was not, in fact, the case. As Wendy Doniger O'Flaherty (1973), one of the great Western scholars of Shiva's symbolism, explains, "The extreme of one force is the extreme of its opposite; *tapas* and *kama,* interchangeable forms of cosmic heat, replace and limit one another to maintain the balance of the universe" (p. 312).

As O'Flaherty (1973) has made clear,

One must avoid seeing a contradiction or paradox where the Hindu merely sees an opposition in the Indian sense—correlative opposites that act as interchangeable identities in essential relationships. The contrast between the erotic and the ascetic tradition in the character and mythology of Siva is not the kind of "conjunction of opposites" with which it has so often been confused. *Tapas* (asceticism) and *kama* (desire) are not diametrically opposed like black and white, or heat and cold, where the complete presence of one automatically implies the absence of the other. They are in fact two forms of heat, *tapas* being the potentially destructive or creative fire that the ascetic generates within himself, *kama* the heat of desire. Thus they are closely related in human terms, opposed in the sense that love and hate are opposed, but not mutually exclusive. (p. 35)

The Indian legends have found various ways of explaining this interrelationship, beginning with a time when the gods, locked in a losing battle with another race called the Titans, propitiated Shiva to come to their rescue, putting his tapas, or spiritual power, to use for their cause. In a last-ditch effort to rouse Shiva from his world-denying meditations, they called on Kama, or Eros, to awaken him to their cause. Shiva was so angry at being disturbed, however, that he incinerated Kama with one glance from his third eye. This eradication of Eros had terrible consequences. The gods realized that without desire the world would be unable to survive. They pleaded with Shiva to bring Kama back to life.

Shiva agreed. He emerged from his meditation and took

the goddess Parvati for his wife. In acquiescing to the pleas of the gods, Shiva committed himself to a yoga that embraced the world, rather than rejecting it. As one of his conditions for joining the fight against the Titans, he instructed the gods that they had to first make peace with their animal natures. Freud would have been proud of him. "I am the Lord of the Animals" (Danielou, 1984, p. 52), he declared, and he made it clear that there was nothing shameful in acknowledging this aspect of one's being. Shiva then took his tapas and turned it toward his lover, uniting with her in a copulation that seemed to last forever.

According to the myths, Shiva and Parvati had sex for more than a thousand years, purely for the sake of sensual pleasure, not to make children. This, too, was an important point. The children that they did create were born in bizarre ways, through a few scrapings of Parvati's skin or the swallowing by a dove of Shiva's semen, after their first sexual relations were long interrupted. Shiva and Parvati's intercourse was pure meditation, the lovers dwelling together in co-generated bliss. Their pleasure *was* the divine state, and it was made possible by the strength of their heat, by the depth of their individual subjectivities.

Passion and restraint, like separation and unity, are two aspects of one energy in Indian wisdom. They exist in dynamic interplay, not seesawing (one going up when the other goes down), but in a more directly proportional relationship in which one can only be fully known through knowledge of the other. Though this is truly a mystical knowledge, it is not outside of our reach. Mannie understood that both psychoanalysis and meditation have the capacity to open the psyche to a place where these correlative opposites can be felt and known.

Healing a Disordered Subjectivity

In addition, Mannie correctly identified the ascetic discipline that has flourished in our time and place as the psychotherapeutic one. He realized that the conclusions of its most seasoned practitioners were remarkably similar to those reached on the Indian subcontinent many centuries ago. As Mitchell (1993) has framed it, the most inspirational clinicians of today have "radically reconceptualized the essence of psychoanalysis from Freud's remedy of exposing, mastering, and renouncing infantile longings to a more broadly conceived project involving a reclamation and revitalization of the patient's experience of self, the healing of disordered subjectivity" (p. 35). Whereas Freud viewed our struggle as being with *unacceptable* impulses, Mannie inspired a more spiritual view of the struggles of the psyche, as a confrontation with the *unintelligible* aspects of our sensual, emotional, and spiritual lives (Phillips, 1995).

The progression from the unacceptable to the unintelligible has real implications for the way in which we approach both spirituality and psychotherapy. To paraphrase Phillips, we can *know* the unacceptable, but we can only *feel* the unintelligible. And we cannot claim the sense of vitality that we crave unless we learn how to feel that which we cannot know, a capacity that both meditation and psychotherapy are capable of encouraging.

> This other unconscious—that which is out of bounds, . . . like the fact of one's infancy, or the fact of one's forthcoming death, or the future itself—is a way of describing both the limits of what we can know and the areas of our lives in which knowing, and the idea of expertise, may be inappropriate.

The unacceptable, to some extent, can be known,
the unintelligible can only be acknowledged. (Phillips, 1995, pp. 16–17)

When Mannie pointed me toward the work of Winnicott, he was instrumental in helping me resolve questions I
had been harboring about the relationship of spirituality and
desire. I found in Winnicott, and in Mannie's reformulation
and explication of his work, the missing piece that linked the
ascetic impulse of meditation to the revitalizing power of authentic desire. In his emphasis on unintegration and play,
Winnicott inspired Mannie to explain, in psychodynamic
terms, what the surrender of meditation was capable of setting
free. Mannie once confided to me that he regretted not going
further in his "Surrender" paper than Winnicott's division of
false self from true self. He knew, by the end of his life, that any
concept of true self had to be false.

Like the incongruous woman in attendance at Ram
Dass's lecture so long ago, Mannie's own craft brought him to
a place where he could experience all of the different aspects of
his psyche as reflections of the whole. He did not need to
position the spiritual at the far end of a continuum that began
with the sexual, nor did he have to reduce the spiritual to its
infantile origins. He was content to keep the process of surrendering alive, opening and opening and opening to the unintelligible and incommunicado aspects of his being. His craft was
not only music, but also psychoanalysis, and at the close of his
"Surrender" paper (1990), he gave a hint of his understanding
of its spiritual dimension:

Let us not overlook the role of masochism and surrender in being a member of our profession. What

other occupation requires of its practitioners that they be the objects of people's excoriations, threats and rejections, or be subjected to tantalizing offerings that plead "touch me," yet may not be touched? What other occupation has built into it the frustration of feeling helpless, stupid and lost as a necessary part of the work? And what other occupation puts its practitioners in the position of being an onlooker or midwife to the fulfillment of others' destinies? It is difficult to find a type of existence, other than that of the psychoanalyst, who fits this job description. In a sense it is the portrait of a masochist. Yet I suspect that a deep underlying motive in some analysts at least, is again that of surrender, and their own personal growth. It may be acceptably couched in masochistic garb or denied by narcissistic and/or sadistic exploitation. When the yearning for surrender is, or begins to be, realized by the analyst, the work is immensely fulfilling and the analyst grows with his patients. (p. 133)

It was my privilege, as it was the privilege of so many others whom he touched, to grow through my association with Mannie. Not confined to the levels of ego, psyche, or even the mysterious "level number three," Mannie was a modern master in an ancient mold, capable of communicating ageless truths in a contemporary voice. I am happy that he called me that day, out of the blue.

Note

1. For a more complete discussion, see *Open to Desire* (Epstein, 2005).

References

Bollas, C. (1987), *The Shadow of the Object: Psychoanalysis of the Unthought Known*. New York: Columbia University Press.

Danielou, A. (1984), *Gods of Love and Ecstasy: The Traditions of Shiva and Dionysus*. Rochester, VT: InnerTraditions.

Epstein, M. (2005), *Open to Desire*. New York: Gotham.

Freud, S. (1910), Five lectures on psycho-analysis. *Standard Edition*, 11: 9–55. London: Hogarth Press, 1957.

Ghent, E. (1990), Masochism, submission, surrender: Masochism as a perversion of surrender. *Contemp. Psychoanal.*, 26: 108–136.

Jung, C. G. (1957), *The Undiscovered Self*. New York: New American Library.

Mitchell, S. A. (1993), *Hope and Dread in Psychoanalysis*. New York: Basic.

—— (2002), *Can Love Last? The Fate of Romance over Time*. New York: W. W. Norton.

O'Flaherty, W. D. (1973), *Siva: The Erotic Ascetic*. Oxford, UK: Oxford University Press.

Paz, O. (1993), *The Double Flame: Love and Eroticism*. New York: Harcourt Brace & Company.

Phillips, A. (1995), *Terrors and Experts*. Cambridge, MA: Harvard University Press.

XII

The Structure of No Structure

*Winnicott's Concept of
Unintegration and the
Buddhist Notion of No-Self*
(2006)

Much of the psychoanalytic fascination with Buddhism stems from the Buddha's assertion of the voidness of self. This is a strong psychological message to be found at the heart of one of the world's most prominent religions, and it has not failed to capture the imagination of psychotherapists, for whom the study of self is a central aspect of their profession. Buddhism affirms a paradoxical truth that psychoanalysis, after one hundred years of investigation, has at times come close to agreeing with: the self which seems so real becomes less so upon analytic inquiry. Where once psychoanalysts seemed sure that the self existed, they now, more often than not, qualify this belief, couching the self in the framework of intersubjectivity, relationality, and relativity. Buddhism, however, has contended from its inception that the self, as we conventionally understand it, is empty of intrinsic reality.

Of course, the problems of language and concept creep immediately into this kind of discussion. What is the self that Buddhism says does not exist? Is this the same self that is explored in psychoanalysis? Is it the self of ego psychology or object relations? Is it the self of healthy or pathological narcissism? A recent review (Falkenstrom, 2003) articulated several different selves that have emerged in the analytic literature of relevance to Buddhist psychology: self as experience, self as representation, and self as system.

The Self That Does Not Exist

Self as experience describes our phenomenological selves: our subjective experience through time. The representational self is an internalized concept of who or what we are, made up of a shifting amalgam of intrapsychic representations that coalesce in varying ways into our repertoire of self-images. And self as system is what might be termed the structure of the self, the architecture or hierarchy of the entire constellation of self-representations. It is a way of talking about the overall shape of an individual person's psychic structure, a description of a person's general capacity for both intimacy and self-awareness.

The Buddhist view of the self that does not exist is relevant, in different ways, at all these levels, although it does not stress any single one of them to the exclusion of the others. It must be remembered that the Buddha's investigation preceded psychoanalysis by twenty-five hundred years and occurred in a culture in which different questions were being asked, and where the notion of soul was much more tied to the concept of self than it is today. Yet given these vast differences in time, place, and culture, it is remarkable how relevant the Buddhist contributions can be to the psychoanalytic model (Epstein, 1995).

In the Buddhist view, all notions of self are held to be potentially imprisoning because of our inherent tendency to cling unproductively to whatever gives a sense of security. This clinging to self may be thought of as a form of narcissism. The Buddha put forth a radical proposition: identification with *any* concept of self, while tempting, is actually unnecessary. It is possible, he declared, to free the mind from its tendency to believe in the ultimate reality of any version of self.

Self as experience is indeed the starting point of the Buddhist investigation, but things get complicated rather quickly when the subjective self is made an object of contemplation. First it becomes obvious that the self that is experienced can be both subject and object. There is experience and the experiencer of the experience, and they are not the same. But then it gets even more complex. As the Buddhist psychotherapist Jack Engler (2003) has pointed out, meditation reveals that there is a source of awareness, consciousness itself, which can never be observed completely in the act of being aware. We can observe it in retrospect and therefore turn it into an object, but we can never truly know it as it occurs. Meditative efforts to observe awareness are always eventually frustrated: the very effort of searching for it removes us from it so that we are always backing up from ourselves, caught in the duality of subject and object. The effort to trap the self ultimately founders on this shore. Self as experience reveals the presence of a self that can never be truly experienced; yet this self, the self of awareness, is clearly an essential and vital aspect of who or what we are. From a Buddhist perspective, observation of self as experience deepens the mystery of our being rather than clarifying it.

On a conceptual level, the sharpening of introspective awareness that takes place in what is known as "insight," or "analytic," meditation brings the various self-representations into focus. Images of self are revealed in all their variety, yet they are also observed to be images rather than reality. They are acknowledged to have a relative reality: they do appear in the mind and can be identified with, but they do not *demand* to be identified with and they are clearly only conceptual in nature. In fact, meditation seems to increase the potential for disidentification from such concepts and, while the self does not become any clearer as a result, the relative nature of the self-representations becomes obvious. The hold that such representations have over us is loosened as an appreciation is gained for an awareness that is vast, ungraspable, and simultaneously immediate and yet out of reach.

Finally, self as system is radically reorganized under the influence of meditation. From one perspective, of course, nothing is changed at all. The self is not destroyed. It is seen to have never existed in any of the ways we imagined. The Dalai Lama compares this realization to that of someone who knows he is wearing sunglasses. The very appearance of the distorted color, he says, is a reminder that what is perceived is not real. On a structural level, the psychologists Daniel Brown and Jack Engler (1986) found that when they gave projective tests to experienced meditators, there was no diminution of internal conflict as compared to controls, only a greater willingness to acknowledge the presence of this conflict. Nothing changes, and yet something is reorganized. Awareness is empowered. The balance between self-observation and self-identification shifts. Narcissistic defensiveness is diminished while the holding power of awareness is strengthened. As identification with the various self-representations fades, awareness fills more and more of the available psychic space.

One important thing to keep in mind in any discussion of Buddhist psychology is that the Buddhist negation of self is not a negation of personhood. In no way does the Buddhist concept of *sunyata*, or voidness, imply that people or things do not exist at all. The etymological root of the word *sunyata*, in fact, has the meaning of a pregnant womb, not of an empty void. *Sunyata* derives from the Sanskrit verb "to swell." It suggests the generative swelling of a seed that contains within it the potential of a whole organism, just as voidness contains within it the diversity of phenomenal existence.

While disputing the reality of an ongoing self with its own intrinsic nature, the Buddha's emphasis on self-observation and self-awareness had the effect of affirming what in today's language is called personal subjectivity (Epstein, 2005). Self as experience was the Buddha's starting place. He was interested, within that vast field, in what could be discovered about the nature of the self as it is directly perceived. This brought him into a deepening exploration of emotional experience, because it is in emotional experience that the self (as we think about it conventionally) becomes most apparent. When we are angry, hurt, anxious, or afraid, or when we really want something or someone, the self comes more into focus. It is a fundamental tenet of Buddhist psychology that in order to understand the emptiness of the "object of negation" (Epstein, 1988), the conventional self must first be seen as clearly as possible. In order to understand voidness of self, we first have to find the self as we experience it. This is one of the primary challenges of Buddhist meditation, at whatever structural level it is practiced.

The Four Noble Truths

The Buddha laid out his psychology in his famous teachings of the Four Noble Truths (Rahula, 1959). His first truth affirmed the presence of a feeling of pervasive unsatisfactoriness. A gnawing sense of imperfection, insubstantiality, or unrest disturbs even pleasurable experiences. He defined aspects of the problem in different ways: (1) Physically, birth, decay, and death are all painful experiences, as are physical and mental illnesses. (2) Emotionally, not to obtain what one desires is suffering; to be united with what one dislikes is suffering; and to be separated from what one likes is suffering. (3) Psychologically, our own selves are troubling. They never seem quite right. There is a discrepancy, as the psychology of narcissism has made clear, between the wishful concept of the self and the self-representations.

The Buddha's second truth gave the cause of dissatisfaction as thirst or craving. He defined three kinds of craving: for sense-pleasures, for existence, and for nonexistence. The thirst for sense-pleasures causes anguish because all such pleasures are fleeting. The objects of our desire are never real enough or lasting enough to give us the ongoing satisfaction that we crave. We are trying to extract an essence from them that they lack, and so we suffer. The thirsts for existence and nonexistence relate to a contemporary understanding of the psychology of narcissism: they can be seen as compensatory self-inflation and compensatory self-negation, the two tendencies of a mind that is searching for certainty in the face of insecurity. This is, in fact, a duality that is typical of both Buddhist psychology and the theories of narcissism. The mind sets up extremes: of existence and nonexistence, absolutism or nihilism, reification or annihilation, or grandiosity and emptiness, and then oscillates among them in a furious attempt to find some solid ground to stand on. In Buddhist psychology, the central motivation for these dualities is "the false idea of self arising out of ignorance" (Rahula, 1959). There is a thirst for certainty, a craving for identity, and a resulting misapprehension of self.

The Buddha's third truth, of cessation, is that there is freedom from unsatisfactoriness. It is possible to extinguish thirst, reconcile polarities, and eliminate false ideas of self. The paradox of the Buddha's psychology, however, is that the only way to accomplish this is to find the self that does not exist. In the Tibetan tradition (Hopkins, 1987) this is described as ascertaining the "appearance of a substantially existent I." In psychoanalytic language, we would call this process an unrelenting excavation of narcissistic identifications. In scanning the field of experience, as is encouraged in Buddhist meditation, the primary focus is on this elusive object: the sense of self as it actually appears. At times, it may be in the form of self-representations; at other times, it may be less conceptual and more of a feeling. However, and whenever, it appears, it is meant to be examined. And this examination yields an appreciation of voidness and a concomitant respect for the mystery of awareness, essential antidotes to the unsatisfactoriness that the Buddha pointed out in his first truth.

The Buddha's fourth truth is the way leading to the cessation of suffering. It is desecribed as the Middle Path, that which avoids the two extremes of indulgence and repression. The former the Buddha desecribed as "low, common, unprofitable and the way of ordinary people," and the latter, which he put in the general category of asceticism, he called "painful, unworthy and unprofitable" (Rahula, 1959). The Middle Path, also known as the Eightfold Path of Right Understanding,

Thought, Speech, Action, Livelihood, Effort, Mindfulness, and Concentration, is designed to highlight and force a confrontation with increasingly subtle psychic manifestations of narcissistic impulses. Meditators, at every stage, have the tendency to use their insights and revelations in a narcissistic manner and to reinforce the sense of their own specialness; one aspect of the path consists of continually uncovering those tendencies in order to reveal the objects of clinging.

As the various self-feelings, self-images, and self-representations are uncovered and observed, there is a corresponding intensification of a commonly overlooked but powerful and mysterious aspect of self: subjective awareness. The effort that Buddhist meditation requires is not just about searching *for* the self, it is also about learning to leave the self alone so that subjective awareness can rise to the surface. This latter effort is toward permitting oneself to simply be, without worrying about keeping oneself together (Epstein, 1998). The appreciation of voidness depends as much on this capacity as it does on the excavation of narcissistic identifications.

Unintegration

Within the psychoanalytic literature, one person whose work clearly dovetails with the Buddhist approach is D. W. Winnicott. Especially in his championing of a state of unintegration, Winnicott gave great credence to the Buddhist suggestion that it could be salutary for the mind to learn how to relax into itself, instead of being caught by all the psychic manifestations of selfhood. But the Buddhist understanding also helps clarify Winnicott's attachment to, and interest in, this state. While Winnicott's descriptions are wonderfully evocative, a careful reading of his work shows him groping for a clear way to express what he found so compelling about an unstructured self. At times equating such a self with madness and at other times with a sacred and "incommunicado" center (Winnicott, 1963), Winnicott's thinking about this matter comes into focus when we read it in the light of Buddhism. In both Winnicott's psychology and that of the Buddha we find the discovery that the less sure we are about the self, the greater is our mental health. Both meditation and Winnicottian psychoanalysis open up uncertainty, not to provoke anxiety but to evoke tolerance, humility, and compassion.

"In thinking of the psychology of mysticism," wrote Winnicott (1963), "it is usual to concentrate on the understanding of the mystic's withdrawal into a personal inner world of sophisticated introjects. Perhaps not enough attention has been paid to the mystic's retreat to a position in which he can communicate secretly with subjective objects and phenomena, the loss of contact with the world of shared reality being counterbalanced by a gain in terms of feeling real" (pp. 185–86). When Winnicott wrote in this way, he was beginning to work out his ideas about a mode of being that he returned to over and over again in his work, one that ties together the worlds of emotional development and meditation. His description is important because of the way he articulates something true about meditation while using the developmental language of psychoanalysis. Communicating secretly with subjective objects is a different, and more accurate, way of describing meditation than is withdrawal into a world of introjects. Meditation opens up subjective experience and makes it into a field of contemplation. It shows us that self as experience is more than the sum of self-representations and that the self as system has to include the unfathomable awareness that illuminates each of us.

"The opposite of integration would seem to be disintegration," said Winnicott (1962). "That is only partly true. The opposite, initially, requires a word like unintegration. Relaxation for an infant means not feeling a need to integrate, the mother's ego-supportive function being taken for granted" (p. 61). Opposing such a state to one of either ego integration or disintegration, Winnicott wrote instead of the importance of relaxing the self's boundaries the way a child can do when he or she knows that the mother is present but not interfering. In Buddhist terms, this remnant of a good enough childhood is also a meditative capacity, one that has to be practiced if it is to flourish but that can eventually open into the freedom of the Buddha's Third Noble Truth.

Unintegration ran through close to thirty years of Winnicott's writings. Introduced in a paper entitled "Primitive Emotional Development" almost as an aside, the concept grew in importance as he integrated it into all the major themes of his work: creativity, feeling real, the true self/false self dichotomy, and the function of therapy. At first, Winnicott's tone was rather sinister: he wrote of unintegration as the underlying truth that we shy away from but are perversely drawn to. At times equating it with a madness that lurks within, Winnicott challenged conventional assumptions of a "healthy" personality that has progressed, evolved, or developed beyond its infantile origins. The healthy individual is not always integrated, declared Winnicott. In fact, it is unhealthy to deny or to fear "the innate capacity of every human being to become unintegrated, depersonalized, and to feel that the world is unreal" (1945, p. 150).

As unintegration came to gather more and more importance in Winnicott's thinking, he began to tie it in more directly to his central notion of the "capacity to be." The infant who can be, as opposed to one who can only do, has the capacity to feel real (Winnicott, 1971). Out of the unintegrated state, she starts to "gather experiences that can be called personal," and she begins "a tendency towards a sense of existing" (Winnicott, 1962, p. 60). As the psychoanalyst Michael Eigen (1991) has written, "Winnicott's therapy created an atmosphere in which two people could be alone together without all the time trying to make sense of what was or was not happening. Developing a capacity for play (transitional experiencing) went along with tolerating unintegration and madness" (p. 78). Or as Winnicott (1971) put it, "The person we are trying to help needs a new experience in a specialized setting. The experience is one of a non-purposive state, as one might say a sort of ticking over of the unintegrated personality" (p. 55).

In this view of therapy we find an immediate overlap with the Buddhist approach. In Buddhism, also, the ticking over of the unintegrated personality is the key to successful practice. Meditation, like Winnicott's psychotherapy, is a way of introducing (or reintroducing) a person to this possibility. In both cases, it is the holding function of awareness that is being developed, sometimes through the participation of the therapist or meditation teacher, and sometimes through the individual's own practice. The self-representations and self-feelings are observed instead of identified with; conflicts are noted without attempts having to be made to solve them. But this holding is not what we usually imagine it to be—it is not a holding on, but more like juggling. Keeping a number of balls in the air, we hold all and none of them. In so doing, the experience of self is opened up, deepened, made more transparent, and transformed.

The scenario I am describing is explored in depth by Winnicott in his penultimate paper, "Communicating and

Not Communicating Leading to a Study of Certain Opposites"
(1963). "In the best possible circumstances," he says, "growth
takes place and the child possesses three lines of communication": (1) communication that is forever silent, which he called
the "incommunicado element" present at the core of each
individual; (2) communication that is explicit, indirect, and
pleasurable, which he linked to verbal and symbolic communications; and (3) an intermediate form of communication
"that slides out of playing into cultural experience of every
kind." When there is a failure, however, and a child is forced to
develop a reactive self to manage the demands of the intrusive
or abandoning environment, "the infant develops a split."
Partly compliant and partly in hiding, the child isolates a secret and impenetrable private world, the remnant of the incommunicado element, to concentrate on managing what we
might call the external world. Christening the split-off dimension a "cul-de-sac communication," Winnicott suggested that
this isolated bubble "carries all the sense of real" (1963, pp.
183–84). Rather than enjoying free access to it in a state of
unintegration, such a person isolates her truest self in an inac-
cessible fortress, hidden even to the self.

The task of the healthy personality is to reestablish contact with this cul-de-sac, to heal the split and open up the
capacity for unintegration that was aborted earlier. The mature person has access to a kind of silent communication that
permits an intensity of personal experience that is lacking
when the thinking mind is always trying to maintain control.

Meditation and Psychotherapy

To me, Winnicott's descriptions of "good enough" parenting
and nonintrusive therapy are powerful evocations of what I

learned, in different language, from meditation. A child who can be lost in play with the knowledge that her parent is present but not interfering is a child who has access to her subjective self. This is a scenario that meditation seems to facilitate. The usual needs for control are suspended, and the self floats. It does not dissolve into nothingness, but it is not maintained in its usual form, either. There is the possibility for silent communication with subjective objects. This temporary dissolution of ego boundaries is both satisfying and enriching, feeding a sense of continuity and trust implicit in Winnicott's notion of what it takes to feel real.

The self that Buddhism finds to be unreal is remarkably similar to the "false self" of Winnicott's psychology. The caretaker self that develops when a child is forced to deal with parental intrusion or abandonment is a self that, in Buddhist language, has no inherent reality. It is a construction, albeit a necessary one at times, that tends to become more and more restrictive the more often it is needed, squeezing the capacity for spontaneity and authenticity into what Winnicott described as a cul-de-sac.

In Buddhist meditation, the dismantling of this false self is encouraged through the deliberate meditative cultivation of unintegration. This is not the endpoint of Buddhism, but it is an important portal of entry. Once comfortable in a state of unintegration, Buddhist psychology contends, we can begin to see clearly how compulsively we cling to the various images of self that present themselves in our minds. Unintegration, the importance of which Winnicott recognized so clearly, is the platform upon which Buddhist insight grows. Without some grounding in it, it is impossible to disidentify enough to see clinging clearly. But when enough subjective expertise is gained, clinging to self becomes very obvious, because it is the clinging itself that disrupts the state of unintegration. From a Buddhist perspective, it is not a single "false self" that is uncovered, however; it is a multiplicity of such selves. The thrill of Buddhist meditation lies in seeing how possible it is to be free of clinging to all such selves, be they experiential, representational, or systematic.

My Buddhist teacher, Joseph Goldstein (1994), tells a story about a moving encounter with one of his teachers that, to my mind, illustrates how central this capacity for unintegration is in both meditative and therapeutic capacities. Joseph was doing a retreat, called a "sesshin," with a very powerful Zen teacher named Sasaki Roshi and was working with a form of meditation known as koan practice, in which he was forced to struggle with a problem, or riddle, that has no rational answer. The sesshin was structured very tightly and Joseph saw the Roshi, or teacher, four times a day for interviews. But each time he tried to solve the koan the Roshi would ring his bell very quickly and dismiss him, saying things like, "Oh, very stupid," or "Okay, but not Zen," leading Joseph to feel more and more ill at ease. Finally the Roshi seemed to relent and he gave Joseph a simpler koan: "How do you manifest the Buddha while chanting a sutra?" Joseph understood that the point was to come in and chant, but it was more complicated than that for him.

As Joseph describes it,

> I do not think Sasaki Roshi knew, although he might have known, that this koan plugged in exactly to some very deep conditioning in me going back to the third grade. Our singing teacher back then had said, "Goldstein, just mouth the words." From then on I have had a tremendous inhibition

about singing, and now here I was, having to per-
form in a very charged situation. I was a total
wreck. In the pressure cooker of the sesshin, which
is held in silence except for the interviews, everything becomes magnified so much.

I rehearsed and rehearsed two lines of chant,
all the while getting more and more tight, more
and more tense. The bell rang for the interview, I
went in, I started chanting, and I messed up the
entire thing. I got all the words wrong: I felt completely exposed and vulnerable and raw. And Roshi
just looked at me and with great feeling said, "Very
good." (p. 21–23)

The therapeutic implications of the encounter were not
lost on Joseph. Sasaki Roshi helped him open up to the very
vulnerability that he was struggling to avoid. By bringing the
false self that developed in the third grade into the meditative
arena, Roshi helped Joseph release himself from its particular
grip. The meditative demands of the koan practice brought that
particular self-representation into the foreground, and its ac-
knowledgment allowed Joseph to deepen his meditation. This
is the model that Buddhist meditation works with. Relaxing
into unintegration empowers an impersonal quality of awareness that takes as its object whatever clinging to self makes a
further opening impossible. Once this obstacle is turned into
an object of meditation, a further release is allowed.

In psychoanalytic language, the change that is brought
about through the cultivation of unintegration is akin to the
empowerment of the synthetic aspect of the ego, that which
must continuously reestablish contact with the object of awareness. This is an aspect of the self, albeit an impersonal one, that

is not weakened by meditation but is strengthened, changing the entire equilibrium of the system conventionally known as self. As the analyst Hans Loewald (1951) has written, "To maintain, or constantly re-establish, this unity . . . by integrating and synthesizing what seems to move further and further away from it and fall into more and more unconnected parts" (p. 14) is the essential aspect of the synthetic function of the ego.

In Buddhist practice, this synthetic ego function is strengthened by meditation. The more comfortable we become in permitting a state of unintegration, the more bits and pieces of self we become aware of. Awareness fulfills its holding function by becoming the swollen and empty container within which the entire process unfolds. Eventually, the still, silent center that Winnicott called incommunicado begins to speak. Sometimes, as Joseph found in his retreat, it even sings.

References

Brown, D., and Engler, J. (1980). The stages of mindfulness meditation: A validation study. Part 1: Study and results. In *Transformations of Consciousness*, K. Wilber, J. Engler, and D. Brown (eds.), Boston: New Science Library, 1986, pp. 161–191.

Eigen, M. (1991). Winnicott's area of freedom: The uncompromisable. In N. Schwartz-Salant and M. Stein (eds.), *Liminality and Transitional Phenomena*, Wilmette, Ill.: Chiron, 1991, pp. 67–88.

Engler, J. (2003). Being somebody and being nobody: A reexamination of the understanding of self in psychoanalysis and Buddhism. In J. D. Safran (ed.), *Psychoanalysis and Buddhism: An Unfolding Dialogue*, Boston: Wisdom, 2003, pp. 35–100.

Epstein, M. (1988). The deconstruction of the self: Ego and "egolessness" in Buddhist meditation. *J. Transpersonal Psychol.*, 20: 61–69.

Epstein, M. (1995). *Thoughts without a Thinker: Psychotherapy from a Buddhist Perspective*. New York: Basic.

Epstein, M. (1998). *Going to Pieces without Falling Apart*. New York: Broadway.

Epstein, M. (2005). *Open to Desire.* New York: Gotham.

Falkenstrom, F. (2003). A Buddhist contribution to the psychoanalytic psychology of self. *Int. J. Psychoanal.,* 84: 1551–1568.

Goldstein, J. (1994). *Transforming the Mind, Healing the World.* New York: Paulist Press, 1994.

Hopkins, J. (1987). *Emptiness Yoga.* Ithaca, NY: Snow Lion.

Loewald, H. W. (1951). Ego and reality. *Int. J. Psychoanal.* 32: 10–18.

Rahula, W. (1959). *What the Buddha Taught.* New York: Grove.

Winnicott, D. W. (1945). Primitive emotional development. In *Through Paediatrics to Psycho-Analysis: Collected Papers,* New York: Brunner/Mazel, 1958, 1992, pp. 145–157.

Winnicott, D. W. (1962). Ego integration in child development. In *The Maturational Processes and the Facilitating Environment,* New York: Int. Univ. Press, 1965, pp. 56–64.

Winnicott, D. W. (1963). "Communicating and not communicating leading to a study of certain opposites," in *The Maturational Processes and the Facilitating Environment,* New York: Int. Univ. Press, 1965, pp. 179–193.

Winnicott, D. W. (1971). *Playing and Reality.* London and New York: Routledge.

XIII
Meditation as Art,
Art as Meditation
Thoughts on the Relationship
of Nonintention to
the Creative Process
(2006)

When I was first learning about Buddhism, I was in college, and I approached it the way I approached most things then. I knew how to go to school and I knew how to study and I figured that I could master meditation the same way I could any other course. I went to a Buddhist summer camp in Boulder, Colorado—a summer *institute*, actually, called Naropa Institute—where any number of scholars and writers and artists and meditation teachers were gathered in what was to be the first of many such summers introducing Buddhism into

Western culture. I took many courses that summer, in Buddhist meditation, psychology, philosophy, and culture while secretly searching for a topic for my upcoming senior thesis in psychology, but I became increasingly frustrated at my failure to master the meditation techniques I was being taught.

My roommates at Naropa, randomly assigned to me by the institute, were twins from Long Island whose parents, Holocaust survivors, ran a fruit and vegetable business in their hometown. These twins took a dim view of most of Naropa's teachers, put off by their self-importance and grandstanding, and, after a bit of time, began making early morning trips to Denver's wholesale fruit and vegetable markets, bringing back cases of fresh cherries, peaches, and other produce that began to fill our townhouse apartment. They watched me in my fruitless pursuit of wisdom until one day one of the twins pulled me aside and offered to teach me to juggle. He handed me a couple of oranges and we got to work. After several days of steady practice, I managed to get the hang of it. Keeping three oranges in the air, I noticed a change in my mind. It was relaxed, yet awake. Open and alert. Not lost in thought, but very aware. My arms moved without me, the oranges orbiting my gaze. Suddenly, all the meditation instruction began to make sense. My introduction to Buddhism was under way.[1] This shift in consciousness is one of the things that links the otherwise disparate worlds of art, therapy, and meditation, three areas of human endeavor where process is as important as product, where the ability to willingly enter psychic territory that most people would rather avoid tends to pay off, where "identity" can be more of an obstacle than an achievement.

Freud was also aware of how helpful this shift can be. In his most explicit instructions to physicians practicing psychoanalysis, he cautioned that the most important method was to simply listen without bothering about keeping anything in particular in mind. Freud was trying to loosen up his followers, to get them to listen with their "third ears" rather than with their thinking minds so that they could make intuitive leaps rather than ponderous progress. The composer John Cage said the same thing in different words in his advice to musicians and composers. He wanted people to listen to all sounds as music, rather than picking and choosing the so-called musical ones. He famously composed pieces of silence, in which the ambient sounds rose to the surface and became a naturally occuring symphony. Cage was trying to free musicians from their ideas of what music was, just as Freud wanted his analysts to listen without trying to fit what they heard into a preexisting schema.

When I first stumbled across Buddhist thought and practice, I did not know very much. I was interested in psychology but found Freud, at that time, to be too difficult, too far outside my own experience to be readily intelligible. Buddhism, on the other hand, spoke clearly and succinctly about my problem. Life is filled with a sense of pervasive unsatisfactoriness, the Buddha proclaimed in his first teachings of the Four Noble Truths. The only way to deal with this dissatisfaction is to learn how not to cling. Changing the way we relate to experience, learning how to not refuse sounds that are not musical, is the key to the Buddha's path. And meditation is the way this change is practiced and learned.

When I met my first Buddhist meditation teachers, I was not yet twenty-one years old. I was good at writing papers and taking tests—I knew how to solve math problems and do research in the library—but in meditation I found something new. I often think that the way I responded to meditation is similar to the way artists feel when first exposed to their craft, one they will make use of for their entire lifetime. Meditation gave me something to throw my whole self into, the way one has to do when painting or taking photographs or making ceramics or playing music. It is a formless art, but one that requires the same diligence, patience, experimentation, immersion, and risk of failure as any other. I was seduced by meditation. It gave me something to engage with, practice, hone my skills with, and explore, and it required everything of me—the more of myself I put into it, and the more I could lose myself in it, the more it gave me back.

The Transfiguration of the Ordinary

When I met my wife, who is a sculptor, it was immediately clear to me that although she did not have a formal meditation practice, her time in her studio was her version of meditation. The way that her process required her to be open to herself, to find a balance between control and surrender, to push into the unknown while being conscious of her reactions but not subservient to them, all spoke of what I knew from meditation. It turns out that this confluence of Buddhist thought and Western artistic process is something that has been of interest to artists since Buddhism was introduced to the West. In this chapter I would like to give some sense of this by tracing one particular arc, one that began in the mid-twentieth century with the travels of D. T. Suzuki, a Japanese writer and lecturer on Zen Buddhism, to New York City. There he gave a series of lectures at Columbia University that were attended by a number of soon to be prominent artists, writers, musicians, critics, psychoanalysts, poets, and philosophers, influencing, in a mostly hidden way, the course of modern art and culture. While the psychoanalysts Erich Fromm and Karen Horney were known to have attended, so did many other aspiring artists of every medium. Let me quote from the philosophy professor and art critic Arthur Danto's description of Suzuki's influence.

> The class met one day a week, in the late afternoon, in Room 716 Philosophy Hall, where departmental seminars were held. There was a very long table. Dr. Suzuki sat at the head of the table, with a blackboard to the left and behind him, though I don't remember him using it. Those who did not find a seat at the table sat in uncomfortable wooden chairs around the wall. In those days, not only was smoking allowed, it was expected. Dr. Suzuki did not, obviously, address hordes. My sense, inevitably vague, is that there would rarely have been as many as forty auditors. Many of those who came were artists, like the sculptor Ibram Lassaw and his wife, or Philip Guston and John Cage, who used to come together. But these are things I learned after the fact. At the time I knew no one who belonged to the Suzuki crowd. Some intellectual historian must one day try to identify the attendees, as has already been done with Alexandre Kojève's course on Hegel, at the College de France. I think Suzuki's course played a role in New York much like Kojève's did in Paris. It helped redirect the way those who were thinkers actually thought. Someone may have kept track of attendance. It would be of interest to know, for example, if J. D. Salinger actually attended, since he is said to have been influenced by Suzuki. Thomas Merton was definitely there.

I cannot pretend to have known Dr. Suzuki himself at all well. He was not an inspiring speaker, however inspired one might have been by his subject matter. He was not especially saintly in manner, but rather urbane, which was just what one might expect, given the values of Zen. But he did look like a Japanese painting of a monk, though he dressed in what is referred to as "business attire" on invitations. Neither was he a witty person, despite his knowledge of koans and what one might term their logic.

From what people told me, Dr. Suzuki kept saying pretty much the same things each time he offered the course—he was, after all, a professor. But that did not keep people from coming back, year after year, to hear it all again. Maybe, in the end, repetition was the point.

I am sure that there were not only artists in Dr. Suzuki's course, but in a way I think I understand what they were after. Let me say, though, that in the 1950s I would naturally have thought in terms of New York School painting when I thought about Zen. Zen went with the gestural way that painters engaged with their work at the time. Today, I can recognize that Zen was more a matter of attitude than performance.

It was not, however, until the 1960s that the wider meaning of what I learned from Dr. Suzuki—if not from his lectures, then from his books—found its way into my philosophy. I would not have been able to see this in terms of 1950s paradigms. The direction of art history itself changed in what I think was a radical way. Whether Dr. Suzuki helped cause this change, or merely contributed to it, is not something anyone can say with certainty. But the people who made the changes were themselves Suzuki's students one way or another. In any case, the meaning of Zen for me came when I had in a way begun to outgrow it.

I am thinking of John Cage and, in particular, of Cage's effort to overcome the differences between music sounds and mere noise. (Danto, 2004, pp. 54–56)

Danto's description helps to set the stage for what I want to present. Suzuki introduced a generation of artists to Buddhist ideas: in particular, to the Buddhist notion that it is possible to train the mind to overcome its usual prejudices, its habits, its conditioning, its preconceptions, and its obsessive preoccupation with language. While appealing to his audience's intellects, Suzuki encouraged them to be suspicious of those very intellects—to find ways of reaching into their unconscious, into the realm of pure subjectivity that we think of as inner space. "But let a man once look within in all sincerity, and he will then realize that he is not lonely, forlorn, and deserted; there is within him a certain feeling of a royally magnificent aloneness, standing all by himself and yet not separated from the rest of existence. This unique situation, apparently or objectively contradicting, is brought about when he approaches reality in the Zen way. What makes him feel that way comes from his personally experiencing creativity or originality which is his when he transcends the realm of intellection and abstraction" (Suzuki, 1960, pp. 30–31).

Suzuki gave his listeners the Zen ball and they proceeded

to run with it. He let them see that they could make art when they took their selves out of the equation, that the cultivation of nonintention did not inhibit creative production but set it free. He laid the foundation for Cage's exploration of chance operations, for Rauschenberg's combines, and for Pop Art's (in Danto's words) transfiguration of the commonplace. This ability to be present while getting the self out of the way is the great discovery that meditation makes possible. We think we are necessary but are startled to find out that we are not.

In Buddhist language, the experience that becomes available when we learn to put ourselves aside is called emptiness, but it is not an empty emptiness or a void, it is rather a full emptiness; the word itself derives from the Sanskrit term for a pregnant womb. As the Buddhist writer Stephen Batchelor has described it, "Emptiness is not a *state* but a *way*. Not only is it inseparable from the world of contingencies, it too is 'contingently configured.'" To experience emptiness is not a descent into an abyss of nothingness nor is it an ascent into a separate realm. It is a recovery of the freedom to configure oneself as an intentional, unimpeded trajectory through the shifting, ambiguous sands of life" (2000, p. 21).

The Music of Changes

This freedom to configure oneself unimpeded by repetitive cycles of obsessive habit is one of the foundations of the artistic process. John Cage listened to D. T. Suzuki's lectures and proceeded to adapt what he heard to the composition of music. He learned to take his own likes and dislikes out of the creative equation so that he could more fully attend to the cycles of nature. "I have always tried to move away from music as an object," he said, "moving toward music as a process, which is without beginning, middle, or end. So that instead of being like a table or chair, the music becomes like the weather" (Nisker, 1986, p. 4). In his later descriptions of his own process, he sounds like a most accomplished teacher of meditation. He managed to forge an integration between art, life, and meditation that has reverberated throughout the culture.

"In the early 1950's," Cage said, after attending two years of Suzuki's lectures at Columbia,

> I began using chance operations to write my music, and after I became acquainted with the *I Ching* (the Chinese Book of Changes), I used it extensively. I apply chance operations to determine the frequency, amplitude, timbre, duration and placement of different elements in my music. The chance operations allow me to get away from the likes and dislikes of my ego, so that I can become attentive to what is outside of my own psychology and memory. By using chance operations I am accepting what I obtain. Instead of expressing myself, I change myself. You might say I use chance operations instead of sitting meditation practice.
>
> I have never engaged in sitting meditation practice. My music involves me always in sitting so that any more sitting would be too much. Furthermore, by the time I came in contact with Zen I had already promised Arnold Schoenberg that I would devote my life to music which is concerned with the sense perceptions. So my meditation has been through my music, where I am trying to get rid of my likes and dislikes and open myself to the flow of experience. (Nisker, 1986, p. 4)

Cage's experiments with what Buddhism calls "bare," or naked, attention had a profound influence on the cultural landscape. In a subtle but irrefutable way, he introduced Buddhist thought into artists' consciousnesses. He opened up the idea of an inner creative process in which artists learn to give way to their art, becoming fluent, as he said, with the life they are living. Listen, for example, to how he influenced the poet John Ashbery's process:

> There have been many times in his life when he felt completely stuck, when the poetry seemed to dry up completely, but the longest and worst began shortly after he graduated from college and lasted more than a year. Then he happened to go to a John Cage concert and heard "Music of Changes"— nearly an hour of banging on a piano alternating with periods of silence, as dictated by a score that Cage had put together using the *I Ching* so that it would be determined by chance rather than by his choice. The music seemed to him to be full of powerful meanings and the idea of composing by chance made him think about writing in a completely different way. It made him want to go right back home and start work. Ever since, he has felt that what he calls "managed chance" is the right method for him.

> Ashbery compares his poems to environments, the idea being that an environment is something that you are immersed in but cannot possibly be conscious of the whole of. They are akin in this sense to environmental art, where, as he puts it, "You're surrounded by different elements of a work

and it doesn't really matter whether you're focusing on one of them or none of them at any particular moment, but you're getting a kind of indirect refraction from the situation that you're in."

This is not modesty—he doesn't want people not to pay attention. Rather, he's trying to cultivate a different sort of attention: not focused, straight-ahead scrutiny but something more like a glance out of the corner of your eye that catches something bright and twitching that you then can't identify when you turn to look. This sort of indirect, half-conscious attention is actually harder to summon up on purpose than the usual kind, in the way that free-associating out loud is harder than speaking in an ordinary logical manner. A person reading or hearing his language automatically tries to make sense out of it: sense, not sound, is our default setting. Resisting the impulse to make sense, allowing sentences to accumulate into an abstract collage of meaning rather than a story or an argument, requires effort. But that collage—a poem that cannot be paraphrased or explained or "unpacked" —is what Ashbery is after. (MacFarquhar, 2005, p. 88)

Night Painting

We can feel the Buddhist influence in Cage in his music, and in Ashbery in his poetry. What about painting? Let me quote from two other artists who attended Suzuki's lectures, artists who configured their own unimpeded trajectories after being introduced to Buddhist thought: Philip Guston and Agnes

Martin, artists who, at first glance, could not be more opposite. First, Philip Guston, lecturing at the University of Min-
nesota in 1978, more than twenty-five years after attending
Suzuki's Columbia lectures:

> I would like to make some comments, but not about
> what my paintings mean. That's impossible, totally
> impossible for me to do. I'm certain that profes-
> sional art writers could do it much better than I
> could. Besides I have developed a tendency to dis-
> believe what artists say in their official statements.
> Nevertheless I will try to be as candid as I can be.
>   I feel that strongly believed in and stated con-
> victions on art have a habit of tumbling and collaps-
> ing in front of the canvas, when the act of painting
> actually begins. Furthermore, I have found that
> painters of my generation are more candid and
> provocative in their casual talk and asides, and fun-
> nier too. Mark Rothko, after a mutual studio visit
> said, Phil, you're the best storyteller around and I'm
> the best organ player. That was in 1957; I still wonder
> what he had in mind. So many articles appeared
> with words like sublime, and noble, and he says he's
> the best organ player around. Franz Kline, in a very
> easy bar conversation in the fifties said, "You know
> what creating really is? To have the capacity to be
> embarrassed." And one of the better definitions
> about painting was Kline's. He said, "You know,
> painting is like hands stuck in a mattress."
>   In a recent article which contrasts the work of a
> colour-field painter with mine, the painter is quoted
> as saying "A painting is made with colored paint on

a surface and what you see is what you see." This popular and melancholy cliché is so remote from my own concern. In my experience a painting is not made with colours and paint at all. I don't know what a painting is; who knows what sets off even the desire to paint? It might be things, thoughts, a memory, sensations, which have nothing to do directly with painting itself. They can come from anything and anywhere, a trifle, some detail observed, wondered about and, naturally, from the previous painting. The painting is not on a surface, but on a plane which is imagined. It moves in a mind. It is not there physically at all. It is an illusion, a piece of magic, so what you see is not what you see.

I think in my studies and broodings about the art of the past my greatest ideal is Chinese painting; especially Sung painting dating from about the tenth or eleventh century. Sung period training involves doing something thousands and thousands of times—bamboo shoots and birds—until someone else does it, not you, and the rhythm moves through you. I think that is what the Zen Buddhists called kensho and I have had it happen to me. It is a double activity, when you know and don't know, and it shouldn't really be talked about. So I work towards that moment and if a year or two later I look at some of the work I've done and try to start judging it, I find it's impossible. You can't judge it because it was felt.

What measure is there, other than the fact that at one point in your life you trusted a feeling.

You have to trust that feeling and then continue trusting yourself. And it works in a reverse way. I know that I started similar things in the past, 20 to 25 years ago, and would then scrape them out. I remember the pictures I scraped out very well, in fact some of them are sharper in my mind than the ones that remained. Well then, I would subsequently ask, why did I scrape them out? Well, I wasn't ready to accept it, that's the only answer. This leads me to another point: it doesn't occur to many viewers that the artist often has difficulty accepting the painting himself. You can't assume that I gloried in it, or celebrated it. I didn't. I'm a night painter, so when I come into the studio the next morning the delirium is over. I know I won't remember detail, but I will remember the feeling of the whole thing. I come into the studio very fearfully. I creep in to see what happened the night before. And the feeling is one of, My God, did I do that? That is about the only measure I have. The kind of shaking, trembling of . . . "That's me? I did that?" But most of the time, we're carpenters, we build and build, and add and prepare and when you drag yourself into the studio, you say, "Oh, that's what I did. It's horrible. All of it has to go." This is one of the last minute touches. Often at the moment you're playing your last card and are ready to give up, another kind of awareness enters and you work with that moment. But you can't force that moment either. You truly have to have given up. And then something happens. (McKie, 1982)

Another kind of awareness. A double activity. Both Guston and Ashbery describe something that meditation makes possible: a kind of attention that emerges when the impulse to make sense is resisted, when feelings of embarrassment are not suppressed, when the random events of ordinary life are noticed rather than screened out, when the proscriptions of language and conceptual thought are circumvented. As Stephen Batchelor describes it in his analysis of a second-century Indian philosopher and poet named Nagarjuna, "As a poet, Nagarjuna gives voice to the freedom of emptiness *from* within. He is not interested in confirming what is safe and familiar, but in exploring what is unsettling and strange; the letting-go of fixed opinions about oneself and the world can be both frightening and compelling. Although such emptiness may seem an intolerable affront to one's sense of identity and security, it may simultaneously be felt as an irresistible lure into a life that is awesome and mysterious" (Batchelor, 2000, p. 24).

From the perspective of the psychotherapist, an analogous method has emerged as the cornerstone of psychoanalytic listening. While it has been cultivated outside the rubric of Buddhist thought, it, too, is predicated on the ability of the mind to attend outside the matrix of linguistic fixation. This is described very clearly by one of Britain's most influential psychoanalysts, W. R. Bion, in a monograph entitled *Taming Wild Thoughts*:

> Freud was extremely impressed with Charcot's statement that when you do not understand a situation, when you cannot perceive what the diagnosis is, you should go on until the obscurity be-

gins to be penetrated by a pattern, and then you can formulate what the pattern is that you see. With regard to ourselves, we are confronted with what seems to be a single individual. Our attention is usually focused on a recently developed capacity of the human being, namely his capacity to elaborate and use articulate speech. It is obviously a very powerful and useful achievement. But while we are in the frame of mind in which it is possible to command the use of relatively recently developed techniques like articulate speech, we also have to contend with the many obscuring words, thoughts, sounds, physical feelings, physical symptoms, in order to excavate the underlying, basic, and fundamental feature. . . .

We do not in fact know who the person is today, tomorrow with whom we are meeting. What we already know and what the patient already knows is of no consequence or importance; the past is past, and anyhow that term is part of the convenience of articulate expression. (Bion, 1997, pp. 35–38)

The Silver Cord

This willingness to be befuddled seems to be one of the most common marks of the enlightened consciousness. You can hear it in Guston's shaking and trembling "That's me?" as well as in Bion's frank admission of ignorance in the face of a seemingly single individual. In the words of Agnes Martin, it shows up in a different form. Martin, who passed away at the end of 2004, was yet another pioneering artist whose vision was irrevocably altered through her attendance at Professor Suzuki's class. She was much more of an ascetic than Guston, or even Cage, but she, too, recognized in her artistic process something akin to the Zen consciousness that Suzuki lectured about. "The intellect is a hazard in artwork," she wrote. "I mean, there are so many paintings that have gone down the drain because somebody got an idea in the middle" (Martin, 1992, p. 165).

> The artist works by awareness of his own state of mind. In order to do so he must have a studio, as a retreat and as a place to work. In the studio an artist must have no interruptions from himself or anyone else. Interruptions are disasters. To hold onto the "silver cord," that is the artistic discipline. The artist's own mind will be all the help he needs.
>
> There will be moving ahead and discoveries made every day. There will be great disappointments and failures in trying to express them. An artist is one who can fail and fail and still go on. (Martin, 1992, p. 93)

> Happiness is unattached. Always the same. It does not appear and disappear. It is not sometimes more and sometimes less. It is our awareness of happiness that goes up and down.
>
> Happiness is our real condition. . . .
>
> When we see life we call it beauty. It is magnificent—wonderful.
>
> We may be looking at the ocean when we are aware of beauty but it is not the ocean. We may be

in the desert and we say that we are aware of the
"living desert" but it is not the desert.

Life is ever present in the desert and every-
where, forever.

By awareness of life we are inspired to live.

Life is consciousness of life itself. (Martin,
1992, pp. 135–136)

There is a way of understanding the making of art that
links the worlds of psychoanalysis and meditation. At its root
is a conception of the unconscious as something other than
just the repository of forbidden libidinal urges. The Buddhist
unconscious, pointed to by D. T. Suzuki in his lectures and
picked up on by Cage, Guston, Ashbery, and Martin, is defined
by its lack of attributes and seeps seamlessly into the mystery
of aliveness. That is why "emptiness" is the safest descriptive
term for it: it is easiest to define by what it is not. The experience of this unconscious is something that meditation aims
for, but it is just as retrievable through the modality of art, or
even psychotherapy. Listen to the contemporary British psychoanalyst Adam Phillips describe his version of it:

Freud's description of the unconscious suggests
that we are lost in thought, and yet people come for
psychoanalysis to find out where, or who, they are.
. . . With the post-Freudian Freud they are likely to
be at cross purposes. Adults, after all, don't tend to
go out with the intention of getting lost (though it's
not obvious why they don't). Nor do people want
to pay good money to realize how clueless they
are. Being all over the place, or being seen to be,
is traditionally considered to be something of a

drawback. Symptoms, like insights—pieces of self-knowledge—at least allow one to identify oneself, to make "I am the kind of person who . . ." statements. But if, as Freud suggests, to "have" an unconscious is to be, or to make oneself radically odd to oneself—to be always in and out of character—what is the analyst supposed to be doing to (or for) his patients? To make them more knowing, or enable them to tolerate, or take pleasure from, their clouds of unknowing? Show them that they are afloat on their ignorance, buoyant sometimes, or help them swim for shore? "To improve society spend / more time with people you haven't / met," John Cage advises. You can't help but do this, Freud says, because the person one hasn't met is also always oneself. (Phillips, 1996, p. 15)

The person one hasn't met is also always oneself. Suzuki was a messenger from another time and place who reminded a generation of this basic truth. The people who heard him most easily were artists. The art that they made, and the artists they in turn have inspired, continues to carry his message, asking us to question ourselves instead of settling into complacency, to open ourselves instead of closing down around what we already know, and to embarrass ourselves instead of worrying what other people think. Artists, like psychoanalysts and Zen teachers, are people who can fail and fail and go on.

Note

1. See Epstein, *Going to Pieces without Falling Apart,* New York: Broadway, 1998.

References

Batchelor, S. (2000). *Verses from the Center.* New York: Riverhead.

Bion, W. R. (1997). *Taming Wild Thoughts.* London: Karnac.

Danto, A. C. (2004). Upper West Side Buddhism. In *Buddha Mind in Contemporary Art,* J. Baas and M. J. Jacob, editors. Berkeley: University of California Press.

MacFarquhar, L. (2005). Present waking life. *New Yorker,* November 7.

Martin, A. (1992). *Writings* (1972–73). Winterthur: Cantz.

McKie, R. (1982). *Philip Guston Catalogue.* London: Whitechapel Gallery.

Nisker, W. (1986). John Cage and the music of sound. *Inquiring Mind* 3, no. 2: 4–5.

Phillips, A. (1996). *Terrors and Experts.* Cambridge: Harvard University Press.

Suzuki, D. T. (1960). Lectures on Zen Buddhism. In E. Fromm, D. T. Suzuki, and R. DeMartino, editors. *Zen Buddhism and Psychoanalysis.* New York: Harper Colophon.

Credits

The author gratefully acknowledges permission to reprint the following material:

Part One: Buddha (Introduction). A portion of this introduction originally appeared in "Analyzing Enlightenment," *Buddhadharma: The Practitioner's Quarterly,* 67–70, Fall 2006. Copyright 2006 by Mark Epstein. Reprinted by permission of *Buddhadharma: The Practitioner's Quarterly.*

Chapter 1, "Meditative Transformations of Narcissism," originally published in the *Journal of Transpersonal Psychology,* 18(2), 143–158, 1986. Copyright 1986 Transpersonal Institute. Reprinted by permission of the *Journal of Transpersonal Psychology.*

Chapter 2, "The Deconstruction of the Self: Ego and 'Egolessness' in Buddhist Insight Meditation," originally published in the *Journal of Transpersonal Psychology,* 20(1), 61–69, 1988. Copyright 1988 Transpersonal Institute. Reprinted by permission of the *Journal of Transpersonal Psychology.*

Chapter 3, "Forms of Emptiness: Psychodynamic, Meditative and Clinical Perspectives," originally published in the *Journal of Transpersonal Psychology,* 21(1), 61–71, 1989. Copy-

Index